ZEKE MAYE

We're Not Fucked

**WINTERS HERE
PRESS**

First published by Winters Here Press 2026

First edition

This book was professionally typeset on Reedsy.
Find out more at reedsy.com

The singularity won't save you

Contents

Introduction

You'll never find me online. You'll only find me in these pages and future books. Online is the devil's work, isn't it? It's the playground of doomscrollers who are plunging us toward the end.

You'll have trouble finding the real me because this is a pseudonym. My presence is only here.

I'm being a bit dramatic, obviously. The internet isn't literally the devil's work but it's just highly effective at making us feel like we're living through the apocalypse when we're mostly just living through Tuesday. I need you to understand why I'm not building a platform, why there's no Instagram account for this book, why you won't find me tweeting hot takes or posting motivational content at 6 AM.

Because I used to be part of the machine that's breaking your brain, and I can't in good conscience participate in it anymore.

My name is Zeke Maye. Well, not really, but that's who I am for you. For real, I spent my twenties as a journalist. Breaking news, developing stories, the constant churn of content designed to capture attention and hold it just long enough to serve you an advertisement. Or pony up for a subscription. I was good at the attention economy. I knew how to write headlines that made you click. I understood the rhythm of outrage that kept you scrolling. I could identify the exact emotional temperature that would make a story go viral.

I thought I was informing people. I thought I was doing important work. I thought staying connected to every crisis, every scandal, every breaking development was what responsible citizenship looked like.

But I was actually just extremely anxious and calling it professionalism.

The breaking point came during what I can only describe as a completely ordinary news cycle, which is to say, it felt like the world was ending but actually it was just a regular week in modern media. I was tracking maybe six different crises simultaneously, refreshing feeds compulsively, monitoring social media for breaking developments, writing and rewriting stories as new information emerged. I hadn't slept properly in days. I couldn't remember the last time I'd had a conversation that wasn't about work. My relationships were deteriorating because I was physically present but mentally somewhere else, always somewhere else, lost in the infinite scroll of human suffering and political chaos.

And then I had what I can only call a moment of clarity, though at the time it felt more like a breakdown. I realized I could tell you intimate details about political scandals in countries I'd never visited, but I couldn't tell you my neighbor's name. I knew the latest celebrity drama, the newest controversy, the most recent outrage! And I knew absolutely nothing about my own life because I wasn't living it. I was consuming other people's curated performances of life while my actual existence atrophied from neglect.

I knew more about distant crises I couldn't influence than about the community I actually lived in. I was "well-informed" in the way that meant I could discuss current events at parties, but I was completely uninformed about things that actually mattered like what my friends were struggling with, what my partner needed from me, what my own values even were underneath all the reactive opinions I'd accumulated.

So I quit. Not just the job, though I did that too, but the entire apparatus of constant connectivity and information consumption. I deleted the apps. I stopped reading news first thing in the morning and last thing at night. I created boundaries around information consumption that felt, frankly, irresponsible given how much was happening in the world.

And you know what happened? The world kept turning without my constant monitoring. Crises continued without my awareness of them. Important events unfolded whether I was watching or not. Somehow, humanity survived my decision to stop doomscrolling.

Meanwhile, something strange happened to me. I started feeling better! Not because the world's problems disappeared, they didn't of course. But because I stopped carrying all of them simultaneously in my nervous system twenty-four hours a day. I started sleeping. I started having actual conversations. I noticed my own life, which it turned out was still there, patiently waiting for me to show up for it.

I also saw how many people around me were where I'd been: drowning in information, marinating in anxiety, convinced that everything was fucked and getting worse, feeling helpless and hopeless and exhausted. Smart people. Good people. People who cared deeply about the world and wanted to make it better but were so overwhelmed by the sheer volume of problems that they were paralyzed, doing nothing except feeling terrible about everything.

And I realized that this isn't just personal dysfunction. This is systemic. We've built information systems that profit from our anxiety. We've created economic structures that benefit from our exhaustion. We've normalized a relationship with media and technology that's literally making us sick while convincing us that this is just what being informed and engaged looks like.

So I started writing this book. Not as an expert. I'm not a psychologist or a neuroscientist or a self-help guru. I'm just someone who fell into the doom spiral, clawed my way out, and wants to throw a rope back to people who are where I was.

This book is that rope.

I'm using a pseudonym not because I'm hiding but because I don't want to build a personal brand around this work. I don't want you following me on social media. I don't want to create another voice you feel obligated to keep up with, another feed you need to check, another source of information competing for your already-fragmented attention.

I want you to read this book, take what's useful, and then close it and go live your actual life. I want these ideas to exist in your practice, not in your parasocial relationship with some author you'll never meet. I want you engaging with your real community, not performing engagement with an online audience.

That's why I'm only here, in these pages. This is the work. Not the platform, not the presence, not the personal brand. Just the ideas and practices and frameworks that might help you navigate difficulty without being destroyed by it.

Here's what this book is: it's twenty chapters of tools, perspectives, and practices drawn from research, philosophy, psychology, and hard-won personal experience. It's a map for getting out of the doom spiral and into something more sustainable. It's not about toxic positivity or pretending everything is fine. That's head in the sand. It's about seeing reality more clearly, which often means seeing that things are both harder and more hopeful than the distorted picture you're getting from your curated feeds.

Here's what this book isn't: a cure-all, a perfect system, a guarantee that if you do everything right you'll never struggle again. Life is genuinely difficult. The world has real problems. You will continue to face challenges. This book won't eliminate that reality. It will help you engage with that reality more effectively, with more resilience, with more meaning and purpose and connection than you're probably managing right now while you're drowning in doomscroll-induced despair.

Some of what's in here will resonate immediately. Some will feel irrelevant or inaccessible. Some will work for a while and then stop working. That's all fine. Take what serves you, leave what doesn't, adapt what needs adapting to fit your actual life and circumstances.

And then, and this is crucial, close the book and practice. Don't just consume these ideas. Don't just add them to your collection of things you've read about self-improvement. Actually do something with them. Start small. Start imperfect. Start wherever you are with whatever you have.

Because here's the central message of everything that follows: you're not fucked. The situation might be difficult. The world might be chaotic. The future might be uncertain. But you're not fucked. You have more agency than you realize, more capacity than you're currently accessing, more possibility than your doom-scrolling brain is letting you see.

This book is about reclaiming that agency, building that capacity, and opening yourself to possibility.

Not through heroic effort or perfect execution. Just through showing up, practicing, adapting, and continuing. Imperfectly, incompletely, but genuinely!

Welcome. I'm glad you're here. Now let's get to work.

—Zeke Maye

1

The Inventory of Doom

Let's start with a thought experiment. Take a moment and make a mental list of everything that's wrong with the world right now. Go ahead, I'll wait.

Don't take too long. I know the tendency is to go down a rabbit hole and stay there about a week, finding every little thing that's wrong with the world. Your world.

You back? Good. Now, how long is that list? Five things? Ten? If you're anything like most people I talk to, you could probably keep going for another four days without even pausing for breath. Climate apocalypse, check. Democracy crumbling, check. Economy teetering, check. AI about to steal our jobs (or destroy humanity, depending on which article you read last), check. And that's just the global stuff before we even get to your personal disasters. The bills, the relationships, the career anxiety, the nagging sense that you're somehow failing at being a functional human being in the 21st century.

Welcome to the Inventory of Doom. Population: basically everyone with an internet connection.

Here's the thing about that mental list you just made. It came to you instantly, didn't it? You didn't have to dig deep or think hard. Those problems were right there, loaded and ready, like apps running in the background of your brain, draining your battery even when you're not actively looking at them.

Now try this instead: Make a list of things that are going right in the world.

Harder, isn't it? Slower. You have to actually *think* about it. And even when you come up with something like medical breakthroughs, renewable energy progress, the fact that you had clean water to brush your teeth this morning, there's this little voice that whispers, "Yeah, but that doesn't *really* count," or "Sure, but it's not enough to matter."

That right there? That's where we need to start. Not with toxic positivity or pretending everything's fine. But with a cold, hard look at how spectacularly we've trained our brains to become connoisseurs of catastrophe.

A Day in the Life of Doomscrolling

Let me paint you a picture. See if it sounds familiar.

You wake up and, before you've even fully opened your eyes, possibly before you've even achieved consciousness in any meaningful philosophical sense, your hand reaches for your phone. It's like your arm is possessed by some doom-seeking demon that operates independently of your rational mind.

The screen lights up. Thirty-seven notifications. Your cortisol spikes before you've read a single word.

You open your news app. The top headline is about some fresh catastrophe. Political scandal, environmental disaster, AI apocalypse, or economic downturn. Take your pick. Your day is twelve seconds old, and you're already anxious. But do you put the phone down? Of course not. You're awake now. Might as well see how bad things *really* are.

You scroll. Each swipe reveals a new flavor of terrible. Conflicts escalating, rights being stripped away, temperatures rising, tensions mounting. Honestly, 30 years ago you wouldn't have known about a rainstorm in California that might cause minor flooding but today it's just another warning from manic meteorologists about climate change. It's like a depressing slot machine, and you keep pulling the lever. Hoping for... what exactly? Good news? A solution? Or just more confirmation that yes, you were right, everything really is going to shit?

Twenty minutes later, you're still in bed, you haven't moved a muscle except your thumb, and you feel like you've already lived through several apocalypses. Your jaw is clenched. Your shoulders are up around your ears. And the day hasn't even started. You don't want to get up.

You finally drag yourself up, make coffee, and open your laptop. Work emails can wait. First, let's check social media. Twitter (sorry, "X," whatever) is on fire about something. Everyone's angry. You're not entirely sure what happened, but the outrage is contagious. You feel your blood pressure rising in solidarity with people you've never met about an issue you learned about forty-five seconds ago.

Facebook shows you that one relative's political post. You know the one. You promise yourself you won't read the comments. You read the comments. You lose faith in humanity a little more.

Instagram reminds you that everyone else is living their best life while you're sitting in your unwashed sweatpants, scrolling through curated highlight reels of other people's vacations, relationships, and perfectly plated breakfasts. Even people's problems look better than yours. At least their mental health struggles are aesthetically pleasing and getting lots of supportive comments.

By lunchtime, you've consumed more crisis content than calories. You've read about seven different ways the world might end, watched three videos of injustice, and absorbed the ambient anxiety of approximately four thousand strangers.

And here's the really fun part. You'll do it all again after lunch. During lunch too. And before dinner. And definitely before bed, because nothing says "restful sleep" like a comprehensive review of everything that's wrong with the world, right?

If this sounds so exhausting, that's because it is. If it sounds familiar, that's because it's basically everyone.

Your Brain on Negativity: A Love Story

Now, before you start thinking you're uniquely broken or weakwilled for falling into this pattern, let me introduce you to your brain. Specifically, the parts of your brain that are, with the best intentions, absolutely sabotaging your mental health.

Your brain is essentially running on software designed for a world that doesn't exist anymore. For most of human history, the humans who survived were the ones who were really, really good at spotting threats. That rustling in the bushes? Could be wind. Could be a tiger. The optimist who assumed it was wind got eaten. The pessimist who assumed it was a tiger lived to have anxious children, who had more anxious children, and eventually, several hundred thousand years later, here you are, treating a push notification with the same level of threat assessment your ancestors reserved for actual predators.

This is called negativity bias, and it's not a bug in your system. It's a feature. Your brain is designed to prioritize negative information over positive information because, evolutionarily speaking, missing a threat was way more costly than missing an opportunity. If you didn't notice that one berry bush, no big deal, there's probably another one tomorrow. If you didn't notice that one leopard, there is NO tomorrow.

The problem is that your ancient threat-detection system can't tell the difference between a leopard and a scary headline. It just knows: DANGER. ALERT. PAY ATTENTION. And because negative information feels more urgent, more important, and more "real" than positive information, your brain keeps pulling you back to it like a moth to a flame. Or, more accurately, like a human to their glowing phone at 2 AM, scrolling through disasters they can do absolutely nothing about.

Research shows that negative news produces stronger and longer-lasting emotional reactions than positive news. We remember bad stuff more vividly. We give it more weight in our decision-making. We talk about it more. One bad thing isn't just equal to one good thing. Damn, it's more like **five** good things. (Some researchers say the ratio is even higher.)

This means your brain is essentially running an accounting system where every positive development counts as one point, but every negative development counts as five to ten points. And then we wonder why it feels like we're losing.

The Algorithm Knows What You're Thinking (And It's Feeding You More of It)

Now, if it were just our brains making us miserable, that would be bad enough. But we've managed to create technology that exploits this vulnerability with terrifying precision.

Social media algorithms are designed with one primary objective: keep you scrolling. Not make you happy. Not make you informed. Not make you a better person. Just keep your eyeballs on the screen so they can sell those eyeballs to advertisers.

And here's what they've figured out! Nothing keeps people scrolling quite like emotional arousal. Fear, anger, outrage, anxiety! These are the feelings that make you unable to look away. They've discovered that if they show you content that triggers your negativity bias, you'll engage more. Click more. Scroll more. Come back more.

So the algorithm learns: "Oh, when I show this person news about climate disasters, they stop scrolling and read. When I show them political outrage, they click through to read the comments. When I show them stories about economic collapse, they share it with their friends."

And what does the algorithm conclude? "Excellent! This person must love climate disasters, political outrage, and economic collapse! Let me show them more of that!"

But you know all this. And yet you just can't stop.

It's like having a butler who notices you nervously picking at a scab and concludes, "Ah yes, my boss enjoys picking at scabs. I shall present them with more scabs to pick." Thanks, butler. Very helpful.

The result is what researchers call "filter bubbles" or "echo chambers." These are personalized reality tunnels where the algorithm shows you more extreme versions of whatever you've engaged with before. If you click on one article about how everything is falling apart, congratulations! The algorithm now believes your deepest passion is watching things fall apart, and it will curate an entire feed designed to convince you that yes, indeed, everything is falling apart, and here are forty-seven more examples.

This creates a weird feedback loop. Your negativity bias makes you notice and engage with negative content. The algorithm notices this and shows you more negative content. This reinforces your sense that everything is negative. Which makes you more likely to engage with negative content. Which tells the algorithm to show you even more of it.

You're not crazy for thinking everything is terrible. You've just trained yourself, with the eager assistance of trillion-dollar tech companies, to only see the terrible parts.

The Outrage Economy

Let's talk about why the news media is the way it is. And by "the way it is," I mean it's seemingly designed by a committee of anxiety demons whose Key Performance Indicator is collective mental breakdown.

News outlets operate on a simple business model. Attention equals money. More viewers, more clicks, more engagement means more advertising revenue. And what captures attention better than anything? Fear and outrage. There's an old saying in journalism we all know: "If it bleeds, it leads." This isn't because journalists are sadists (well, not *most* of them). It's because decades of data have shown that people pay more attention to negative news. A story about a local crime spree gets more viewers than a story about declining crime rates. A headline about economic collapse gets more clicks than a headline about steady growth.

So media outlets, even well-intentioned ones, are economically incentivized to emphasize the negative. Not necessarily to lie, but to frame, select, and present information in the most attention-grabbing way possible. Which usually means the most alarming way possible.

This creates what some researchers call "mean world syndrome." That's when people who consume a lot of news start believing the world is more dangerous, more violent, and more negative than it actually is. Their perception of reality becomes skewed not because they're stupid or gullible, but because they're consuming a highly curated, unrepresentative sample of what's actually happening in the world.

Think about it. A plane crashes, and it's international news for days. Tens of thousands of planes land safely every single day, and you hear nothing about it. Why would you? "Plane Lands Fine, Just Like All the Other Planes" isn't exactly a compelling headline. But the result is that we dramatically overestimate how dangerous air travel is because our information diet consists entirely of the exceptions, not the rule.

The same thing happens with everything else. Violent crime might be declining, but if the news reports every violent crime that occurs, your brain concludes, "Wow, there sure is a lot of violent crime." A hundred studies might show progress on climate solutions, but the one scary prediction about worst-case scenarios is what makes headlines.

None of this is to say that real problems don't exist. They absolutely do. But we're getting a deeply distorted picture of the ratio of problems to non-problems, which leaves us feeling like we're drowning in a sea of catastrophe. When reality is more complicated than that.

The Story We Tell Ourselves

Here's where things get really wild. By wild, I mean "potentially life-changing if you're willing to examine it."

All of this external stuff: the negativity bias, algorithms, and media landscape, they're real and they matter. Not gonna lie. But none of it would have such power over us if we weren't actively participating in our own doom narrative.

Because here's the uncomfortable truth. On some level, we're choosing this.

I know, I know. You're thinking, "Choosing? I'm not *choosing* to feel like everything is falling apart. I'm *observing* that everything is falling apart. Big difference."

But is it? Because I'm willing to bet that alongside all the genuinely terrible things happening in the world, there are also good things happening. People helping each other. Problems being solved. Progress being made. Small kindnesses and major breakthroughs and ordinary moments of beauty and connection.

And we're not paying attention to those things. Not because they don't exist, but because they don't fit the narrative we already believe that everything is fucked, we're fucked, and anyone who suggests otherwise is naive, lying, or trying to sell you something.

This narrative becomes a lens through which we filter all incoming information. Good news? Must be temporary, or fake, or somehow actually bad news in disguise. Someone's optimistic? They must not understand how bad things really are. Things working out? Just wait, it'll fall apart soon enough.

Psychologists call this "confirmation bias." It's our tendency to notice, seek out, and remember information that confirms what we already believe, while dismissing or forgetting information that contradicts it. Combine confirmation bias with negativity bias, add a dash of algorithm-fueled echo chamber, and you've got a recipe for profound, unshakeable conviction that everything is terrible and getting worse.

And here's the really insidious part! This belief becomes self-fulfilling. When you believe everything is fucked, you stop trying. Why bother? When you believe your actions don't matter, you don't take action. When you believe the world is spiraling into chaos, you retreat from it rather than engaging with it. And all of that creates more of the very hopelessness that convinced you everything was fucked in the first place.

It's like being in a relationship where you've convinced yourself your partner is definitely cheating on you. Every piece of evidence gets interpreted through that lens. They came home late? Cheating. They're being extra nice? Guilty conscience, obviously. They're being distant? See, I knew it. And because you're now acting suspicious, jealous, and withdrawn, you're actually damaging the relationship, creating the very distance and dysfunction you feared. Regardless of whether they were actually cheating.

We're doing that with reality. We've decided the relationship is doomed, and so we're interpreting everything through that lens, and our interpretation is making us act in ways that create more doom.

The Question That Changes Everything

So here we are. You've made your Inventory of Doom. You've recognized the patterns of doomscrolling. You understand that your brain is biased toward negativity, that algorithms are exploiting that bias, that media profits from your anxiety, and that you're potentially trapped in a self-fulfilling prophecy of despair.

This is where most books would try to cheer you up with some uplifting quotes or dubious statistics. But we're not doing that here. Because pretending everything is fine when you genuinely believe it's not is about as useful as putting a "Live, Laugh, Love" poster over a hole in your wall. Sure, it's covering something up, but the structural damage is still there.

Instead, I want to leave you with a question. Not a comfortable one. An uncomfortable, slightly threatening one that might make you defensive. Ready?

What if the story you're telling yourself isn't the whole story?

What if your perception of reality has become more distorted than reality itself?

What if you've become so fluent in the language of disaster that you've forgotten how to recognize anything else?

What if, and stay with me here, what if you're actually wrong about how fucked everything is?

Not wrong that problems exist. Not wrong that things are hard. Not wrong that bad stuff is happening. But wrong about the totality of it. Wrong about the trajectory. Wrong about the possibilities. Wrong about your own powerlessness in the face of it all.

What if you've trained yourself to see only the terrible, and that trained perception has convinced you that terrible is all there is?

I'm not asking you to believe me right now. I'm not asking you to suddenly become optimistic or to pretend away your concerns. I'm just asking you to hold open the possibility, and just a crack for now, that the story might be more complicated than the one you've been telling yourself.

Because here's the thing: if you're wrong about being fucked, if things are actually more nuanced than your doom spiral suggests, then you've been putting yourself through enormous unnecessary suffering. You've been living in a mental prison of your own construction, and the door might not actually be locked.

And if there's even a chance that's true, wouldn't you want to find out? Of course you would.

The rest of this book is about finding out. Not through denial or delusion, but through honest examination of how we perceive, interpret, and engage with reality. We're going to look at the architecture of your mind, the actual state of the world (which might surprise you), and the practices that can help you see more clearly.

We're going to figure out how to be realistically optimistic in a world with real problems. How to stay engaged without being consumed. How to maintain hope without ignoring difficulty. How to take meaningful action instead of drowning in helplessness.

But first, you had to see the pattern. You had to recognize how thoroughly you've trained yourself to expect the worst. You had to take inventory of your doom.

Consider it taken.

Now let's figure out what to do about it.

2

The Architecture of Your Mind

Pop quiz: Are you reading this book, or is this book reading you? Too soon for a mind bending question?

Before you dismiss that as pseudo-philosophical nonsense, consider this: Right now, your brain is taking symbols on a page (or screen), converting them into electrical signals, interpreting those signals based on your prior experiences, expectations, and current emotional state, and finally constructing something called "meaning" that exists nowhere except inside your skull. You think you're passively receiving information, but you're actually actively creating your experience of reality, word by word, moment by moment.

Your brain isn't a camera that objectively records what's happening. It's more like a film director, editor, and special effects team all working together. It's deciding what to film, what to cut, what to emphasize, and what story to tell with the footage. And here's the kicker. You don't even realize you're doing it. You just watch the finished film and think, "Yep, that's reality."

Except it's not. It's your brain's interpretation of reality, which is a very different thing.

And if you've spent years training your brain to interpret everything through a doom-tinted lens.

Well, buckle up, because we're about to take a tour of your mental architecture and figure out why you've accidentally constructed a house of horrors when you could have been building something a lot more livable.

Your Brain Is Not Objective (And That's a Problem)

Let's start with an uncomfortable truth. You have no direct access to reality.

I know this sounds like something a philosophy major would say at 3 AM after too many edibles, but it's actually just neuroscience. Everything you experience including every sight, sound, thought, and feeling is filtered through your brain's interpretation systems before it reaches your conscious awareness. You're not experiencing the world. You're experiencing your brain's best guess about the world, based on incomplete information and some pretty questionable assumptions.

Think of your brain like an assistant who's supposed to give you a briefing on what's happening. Except this assistant has some strong opinions, a selective memory, and a tendency to editorialize. You ask for the facts, and they give you the facts, sort of. Plus their interpretation, plus what they think you want to hear, plus what they're worried about, all blended together so smoothly that you can't tell where the objective information ends and their editorial spin begins.

This is why two people can witness the exact same event and come away with completely different stories about what happened. It's not that one is lying (necessarily). It's that each brain is running its own interpretive process, filtering reality through different expectations, beliefs, fears, and biases.

And those biases? Oh boy, do we have biases. Even you. And me.

The Mental Shortcuts That Are Screwing You Over

Your brain is lazy. Not in a bad way. It's actually being efficient.

Processing all the information coming at you every second would require massive amounts of energy, so your brain has developed shortcuts, called cognitive biases, to help you make quick decisions without burning through calories like a supercomputer.

These shortcuts worked great when you were a hunter-gatherer trying not to get eaten by a tiger. They work considerably less great when you're a modern human trying not to have a panic attack in the middle of Target.

Let's talk about some of the greatest hits in your brain's collection of self-sabotage:

Confirmation bias is your brain's tendency to seek out, notice, and remember information that confirms what you already believe, while conveniently ignoring or forgetting information that contradicts it. Remember that narrative we talked about in Chapter 1? The one where everything is fucked? Confirmation bias is how that narrative stays alive even when evidence suggests otherwise.

You believe the world is getting worse, so you notice every news story about crime, corruption, and climate disaster. These stories confirm your belief, which strengthens your conviction, which makes you more likely to notice similar stories in the future. Meanwhile, stories about progress, solutions, and positive developments barely register. And if they do register, you immediately explain them away: "Sure, but that won't last," or "That's just one example," or "They're probably lying about the data."

Your brain isn't doing this to mess with you. It's trying to create a coherent worldview, which require consistency. Contradictory information threatens that coherence, so your brain protects you from the discomfort of cognitive dissonance by simply not letting the contradictions in.

The availability heuristic is your brain's tendency to judge how common or likely something is based on how easily you can recall examples of it. If you can quickly think of several plane crashes, your brain concludes that plane crashes must be pretty common. Even though you can easily recall them precisely because they're rare and therefore newsworthy.

This is why living in the age of 24/7 news and social media is such a minefield for your mental health. You're constantly exposed to dramatic negative events from around the world, which makes your brain think dramatic negative events are happening constantly. The fact that you're seeing more examples isn't because more bad things are happening. Nope. It's because your access to information has expanded exponentially. But your brain didn't evolve to make that distinction.

Catastrophizing is your brain's impressive ability to take any situation and imagine the worst possible outcome, then treat that imagined outcome as if it's not just possible but probable, or even inevitable. It's the "if this, then that, then that, then we're all doomed" chain of reasoning that spirals from "I made a mistake at work" to "I'll definitely get fired" to "I'll never get another job" to "I'll die alone and homeless" in about thirty seconds.

Again, this made sense evolutionarily. The humans who assumed the worst-case scenario and prepared for it were more likely to survive than the optimists who got blindsided by disaster. But now you've got a brain that treats every work email with a vague subject line like it's a saber-toothed tiger.

The beautiful irony here is that we're using mental shortcuts designed to help us survive in order to convince ourselves we won't survive. We're using threat-detection software to detect threats that largely don't exist, which creates real threat (anxiety, stress, cortisol) in our bodies, which our brains interpret as evidence that we were right to be worried, which reinforces the whole cycle.

Your brain is basically gaslighting you, but it's doing it with the best intentions.

Neuroplasticity: Your Brain Is Not Stuck

Here's the good news that might actually change your life if you let it. Your brain is not in a fixed state.

For a long time, scientists believed that brain development stopped in early adulthood and that was it. You've got the brain you got, and you had to live with it. Pessimistic? Anxious? Depressed? Sorry, that's just your personality now. Better luck in the next life.

Turns out, that's spectacularly wrong.

Your brain has this quality called neuroplasticity. It's the ability to form new neural connections and reorganize existing ones throughout your entire life. Every time you think a thought, feel an emotion, or engage in a behavior, you're strengthening certain neural pathways and weakening others. Your brain is constantly rewiring itself based on what you focus on and how you engage with the world.

Think of it like this: Your brain is a forest, and your thoughts are paths through that forest. The more you walk a particular path, the more worn and easy to walk it becomes. Eventually, you've got this super-highway of a path that you can walk without even thinking about it. That's a habit, a neural pathway that's been reinforced through repetition.

If you spend years walking the "everything is terrible" path, that becomes your default route. Your brain gets really efficient at catastrophizing, at finding threats, at generating anxiety. Not because you're broken or weak, but because you've practiced those patterns so many times that they've become automatic.

But, and this is the crucial part, if you've trained your brain to default to negativity, you can retrain it to default to something else. Those neural pathways aren't permanent structures; they're more like trails that grow over if you stop using them. You can deliberately create new paths and walk those instead until they become the new defaults.

This isn't wishful thinking or self-help pseudoscience. This is observable, measurable brain change. Studies have shown that practices like mindfulness meditation, cognitive behavioral therapy, and gratitude exercises literally change brain structure. They strengthen areas associated with emotional regulation and positive emotion while reducing activity in areas associated with anxiety and stress.

Your pessimism isn't a personality trait you're stuck with. It's a learned pattern. And learned patterns can be unlearned.

The RAS: Your Brain's Bouncer

Let me tell you about one of the most important parts of your brain that you've probably never heard of: the reticular activating system, or RAS.

The RAS is basically the bouncer at the club of your conscious awareness. Every second, your senses are bombarded with approximately eleven million bits of information. Eleven million. There is no possible way your conscious mind could process all of that, so your RAS filters it down to about forty bits of information that actually make it through to your awareness.

That means you're consciously experiencing about 0.0004% of available information at any given moment. The other 99.9996% gets filtered out before you even know it exists.

Now, here's the critical question. How does your RAS decide what gets through and what gets filtered out?

It lets through information that's relevant to your current goals, beliefs, and survival. If you're hungry, you suddenly notice every restaurant. If you're thinking about buying a specific car, you suddenly see that car everywhere, even though the number of those cars on the road hasn't actually changed. Your RAS has decided that information is now relevant, so it's letting it through.

The same thing happens with threats and negativity. If your brain believes the world is dangerous and falling apart, your RAS prioritizes threat-related information. You notice every concerning headline, every example of dysfunction, every reason to worry. Not because that's all that exists, but because that's what your RAS has been instructed to look for.

Remember that thought experiment from Chapter 1 where making a list of what's wrong was easy, but making a list of what's right was hard? That's your RAS in action. You've trained it to prioritize negative information, so that's what breaks through into your awareness. The positive information is still there, of course. You're just not seeing it because your RAS has been told it's not relevant to your current worldview.

Here's the wild part! You can retrain your RAS. You can deliberately shift what you focus on, and over time, your RAS will adjust its filters accordingly. This isn't about forcing positivity or ignoring problems. It's about recognizing that your current filter settings are giving you a wildly unbalanced view of reality, and you have the power to adjust them.

Start noticing examples of kindness, and you'll start seeing kindness everywhere. Not because the world suddenly got kinder, but because your RAS has learned to let that information through. Start looking for solutions instead of just problems, and you'll be amazed how many solutions become visible.

Your RAS isn't creating reality. It's determining which slice of reality you get to experience. And you have way more control over that than you think.

Attention as Currency

We talk about "paying" attention, and that's actually more accurate than we realize. Attention is a currency. It's a limited resource that you spend throughout the day. And like any currency, where you spend it matters enormously.

The quality of your life is largely determined by what you pay attention to. Not what happens to you, but what you choose to focus on in what happens to you.

You could have a day where ninety-nine things go right and one thing goes wrong, but if you spend all your attention on the one thing that went wrong, you'll end the day feeling like it was a terrible day. Your experience of reality will be negative, even though the objective reality was overwhelmingly positive.

Now, before you start thinking this is victim-blaming or suggesting that people in genuinely difficult situations can just "choose" to be happy, let me be clear: This is not about toxic positivity or pretending suffering doesn't exist. Bad things are real. Injustice is real. Pain is real.

But, and this is crucial! Even in difficult circumstances, where you direct your attention matters. You can acknowledge pain while also noticing resilience. You can recognize injustice while also seeing resistance and solidarity. You can experience difficulty while also appreciating support, growth, or meaning.

This is the difference between awareness and obsession. Between being informed and being consumed.

Awareness means you know about problems, you understand their reality and significance, and you can respond appropriately. **Obsession** turns into you can't stop thinking about problems even when thinking about them isn't helping anyone, including yourself.

Being informed means you have enough knowledge to make good decisions and take meaningful action. **Being consumed** turns into you're drowning in information to the point where you're paralyzed and depleted.

Your attention is powerful, and the modern world is designed to steal it from you. Every app, every website, every notification is engineered to capture and monetize your attention. If you don't actively decide where your attention goes, corporations and algorithms will decide for you! And I promise you, they don't have your wellbeing in mind.

The Complacency Question

Okay, I know what you're thinking. Maybe you've been thinking it since Chapter 1, or maybe it just crystallized now, but here it is: "If I stop focusing on how bad things are, won't I become complacent? Won't I stop caring about important problems? Isn't my anxiety and outrage actually necessary to motivate action and change?"

This is a genuinely important question, and it deserves a genuinely thoughtful answer, not some dismissive "just chill out" nonsense.

Here's the truth: No, focusing on the negative doesn't make you more effective at solving problems. If anything, it makes you less effective.

Chronic negativity, anxiety, and doomscrolling don't motivate constructive action. They enable paralysis, burnout, and despair. When you're overwhelmed by how bad everything is, you're not energized to fix things. You're exhausted before you even start. You're not strategically addressing problems; you're reactively freaking out about them.

Real change requires sustained energy, strategic thinking, creativity, collaboration, and hope. All of those things are incompatible with the mental state created by constant catastrophizing and doom consumption.

Think about the most effective activists, organizers, and change-makers you know or have read about. Are they the ones who are paralyzed by despair and constantly talking about how fucked everything is? Or are they the ones who clearly see problems but maintain enough hope and energy to actually do something about them?

Seeing reality clearly, including both challenges and opportunities, isn't complacency. It's the opposite. It's the foundation for effective action.

Complacency is thinking everything is fine and there's nothing to do. Realistic optimism is thinking things are challenging but changeable, and there's plenty to do, and doing it might actually matter.

Your current approach, marinating in negativity, isn't keeping you engaged. It's keeping you depleted. And depleted people don't change the world. They collapse on the couch and doomscroll until bedtime.

Seeing Clearly

So what does it actually mean to "see reality clearly"?

It means developing the ability to hold multiple truths at the same time. Things can be both difficult and manageable. Problems can be both serious and solvable. The world can be both challenging and improving. You can be both aware of suffering and capable of joy.

You need to recognize that your current perception isn't objective reality but rather one possible interpretation of reality. It's an interpretation that's been heavily influenced by cognitive biases, algorithmic manipulation, media economics, and your own practiced patterns of attention.

When you say "I'm just being realistic," what you often mean is "I'm being consistently pessimistic and calling it realism." Actual realism includes the full picture including the problems and the progress, the challenges and the opportunities, the suffering and the flourishing.

You need to accept that you have tremendous power over your own experience through where you direct your attention and how you interpret what you encounter. It's not unlimited power over circumstances, but real power over perception and response.

And it means recognizing that the architecture of your mind is not a prison you're stuck in. It's more like a house you've been living in for so long that you forgot you could renovate. The walls can be moved. The lighting can be changed. The view from the windows can be expanded. Your brain has been trained by evolution, experience, modern media, and your own repeated patterns to default to negativity. And now you understand why. Negativity bias, confirmation bias, availability heuristic, catastrophizing, RAS filters set to threat mode, "and results in attention spent primarily on what's wrong.

But here's what changes everything! If your brain can be trained toward negativity, it can be retrained toward balance. If neural pathways can be carved through repetition of destructive patterns, new neural pathways can be carved through repetition of constructive ones. If your RAS can be set to filter for threats, it can be reset to filter for a more complete picture.

You won't become delusional or ignore reality. You'll first recognize that the reality you're currently seeing is already distorted. It's bent toward the negative. Only seeking balance will actually get you closer to truth, not further from it.

You built this architecture. You can rebuild it.

And in the chapters ahead, we're going to learn exactly how.

3

The Truth About Progress

I used to be absolutely certain that the world was going to hell.

Not in a casual "things are rough" kind of way, but with the fervent conviction of someone who had done their research, examined the evidence, and arrived at the only rational conclusion: we were fucked, collectively and individually, and anyone who suggested otherwise was either ignorant or selling something.

I had my arguments ready. Climate catastrophe: check. Rising authoritarianism: check. Economic inequality spiraling out of control: check. Erosion of truth and reason: check. Social fabric tearing apart: check. I could rattle off statistics, cite articles, point to trends. I was, I believed, one of the informed ones. A former journalist, someone who had the courage to look directly at how bad things really were.

And then one day, someone challenged me with a simple question: "Compared to when?"

I was ready to argue. "Compared to, you know, before. When things were better."

"When exactly was that?" they pressed. "The 1950s? The 1800s? The Middle Ages? When specifically was this golden age you're comparing

28

the present to?"

I opened my mouth to answer and realized I didn't actually have one. I had this vague sense that things used to be better. Yeah, more stable, more hopeful, more functional. But I couldn't point to a specific time period that was objectively superior to now across the board. The 1950s had nuclear brinkmanship and segregation. The 1800s had colonialism and child labor. Go back further and you get plague, tyranny, and a life expectancy of about thirty-five years.

That conversation planted a seed that eventually grew into something that changed how I see the world. Not because I stopped caring about problems. Oh, I care about them more than ever. But because I started asking a different question: What if my perception of decline isn't based on actual decline, but on a cognitive bias that makes decline feel more real than progress?

What if I'm wrong about how wrong things are?

The Data Doesn't Care About Your Feelings (Or Mine)

Let's talk about something that's going to make you uncomfortable, possibly angry, and maybe even skeptical that I'm not secretly a corporate shill or dangerously naive optimist.

By almost every measurable metric, the world is better now than it has ever been in human history.

I know. I felt my whole body resist those data points. Everything in me wanted to argue, to list exceptions, to explain why this couldn't possibly be true. But here's the thing about data. It doesn't care about our feelings or our narratives. It just is.

Let's start with **poverty**. In 1820, roughly 90% of humanity lived in extreme poverty. As of 2020, that number is below 10%. Read that again: We've gone from nine out of ten people living in extreme poverty to fewer than one in ten. In 200 years, we've pulled billions of people out of the most desperate conditions of human existence.

29

Child mortality: In 1800, about 43% of children died before their fifth birthday. Today, that number is below 4%. If you're a parent reading this, imagine flipping a coin every time you had a child to determine if they'd live to age five. That was normal for most of human history. Now it's rare enough that when it happens, it's considered a tragedy rather than an expected part of life.

Literacy: Two centuries ago, only about 12% of the world's population could read. Today, it's over 86%. We've gone from literacy being a privilege of the elite to illiteracy being the exception.

Life expectancy has more than doubled globally in the past 150 years. Smallpox has been eradicated. Remember smallpox? It's a horrible disease that killed 300 million people in the 20th century alone and no longer exists outside of laboratories. Polio is nearly gone. Guinea worm disease went from 3.5 million cases in the 1980s to fewer than 50 cases in recent years.

Violence has declined dramatically. Wars are less frequent, less deadly, and affect smaller portions of the population than at any point in recorded history. Murder rates in most of the world have plummeted. Judicial torture, once routine, is now globally condemned.

More people live in democracies than ever before. In 1900, not a single country had universal suffrage. Today, more than half the world's population lives in democracies with elected governments.

I could go on. Clean water access, vaccination rates, educational attainment, reduction in hunger, declining rates of discrimination based on race and gender, technological advances that would seem like magic to someone from even fifty years ago etc etc. The list is long and the progress is real.

Why Progress Feels Impossible

So if things are genuinely getting better by most measurable standards, why does it feel like we're living through civilizational collapse?

Welcome back to your brain's greatest hits of cognitive dysfunction. First, there's what psychologists call the *availability heuristic*, which we touched on in Chapter 2. We judge how common something is by how easily we can recall examples. A plane crash is vivid and memorable; millions of safe flights are not. A horrific crime dominates the news cycle; declining crime rates over decades barely get mentioned. Our brains conclude that plane crashes and violent crime are common because we can easily remember examples, even though we're remembering them precisely because they're rare enough to be newsworthy.

Second, there's *negativity bias on steroids*. Bad news is sudden and dramatic. A building collapses, a war starts, a pandemic emerges. Good news is usually gradual and incremental. Poverty rates decline by 2% per year, child mortality drops slowly but steadily, literacy increases generation by generation. Our brains are wired to notice sudden changes (potential threats) and ignore gradual changes (probably fine, we'd notice if something was wrong).

This is why you can have 99 things improve slowly over decades and one thing get suddenly worse, and the headlines, your attention, and your overall sense of how things are going will all focus on the one thing that got worse.

Third, there's the *Euphemistic Treadmill of Outrage*. As things improve, our standards for what we consider acceptable problems rise. This is actually good. It means we're not settling. Still, it creates the illusion that things are getting worse even as they're getting better.

Example: Fifty years ago, domestic violence was widely considered a private family matter. Today, we recognize it as a serious crime and social problem. Does this mean domestic violence has increased? No, it's actually decreased. But our awareness and naming of it has increased, making it feel like a growing crisis even as the actual incidence declines.

Same with many forms of discrimination. We're more aware of and less tolerant of behaviors that were once considered normal, which creates the impression that things are getting worse when actually our standards are getting better.

Fourth, *media economics amplify negativity*. As we discussed in Chapter 1, news outlets make money from attention, and nothing captures attention like fear and outrage. You're far more likely to hear about one violent crime than about the statistical reality that violent crime has declined dramatically in most developed nations over the past thirty years.

And finally, there's good old *declinism*, which is the persistent belief that things are always getting worse. That appears to be a nearly universal human cognitive bias. Surveys show that in virtually every country, the majority of people believe their nation is in decline, things were better in the past, and the future looks bleak. This has been true in survey data going back decades, even during periods of measurable improvement.

We seem to be hardwired to believe in decline. Which means our sense that everything is getting worse is probably not reliable evidence that everything is actually getting worse.

"But What About..."

Okay, I hear you. You're mentally composing a list of objections right now. You're thinking, "Sure, but what about climate change? What about rising authoritarianism? What about inequality? What about [insert the specific crisis you're most worried about]?"

These are legitimate questions, and they deserve real answers, not dismissive hand-waving.

Here's the truth: Yes, we face serious problems. Climate change is real and urgent. Inequality has increased in many countries. Democratic backsliding is occurring in some nations. Antibiotic resistance is a growing concern. Mental health challenges appear to be rising, particularly among young people.

All of that is true. And here's what's also true: The world can be both better than it's ever been and still have serious problems that need addressing.

This isn't a contradiction. It's reality.

Think of it like your health. You could be in the best shape of your life. Stronger, more fit, healthier habits than you've ever had. And still have a problem that needs attention. Maybe you've developed high blood pressure. That's a real issue that requires real intervention. But it doesn't negate all the progress you've made. You don't say, "Well, I have high blood pressure, so I guess all that exercise and healthy eating was pointless." You address the blood pressure while maintaining those healthy habits.

The same is true at a global scale. We can acknowledge that humanity has made extraordinary progress while also recognizing that we face new and ongoing challenges. Progress in one area doesn't cancel out problems in another. They coexist.

Here's what changed for me. I realized that my all-or-nothing thinking—"if everything isn't perfect, then everything is fucked"—was actually making me less effective at addressing the problems I cared about.

When I believed everything was irredeemably broken, I was paralyzed. Why try? Why engage? Why take action when the whole system is collapsing? My despair felt righteous and informed, but it was actually just despair. It wasn't motivating me to do anything except feel terrible and doom-scroll.

When I started recognizing actual progress while still acknowledging real problems, something shifted. I could see that human action had made things better in the past, which meant human action could make things better in the future. Problems became challenges to address rather than evidence of inevitable doom. I became more engaged, not less. More motivated to contribute to solutions, not paralyzed by the scope of the problems.

Recognizing progress doesn't make you complacent. If anything, it makes you more effective because you can see that effort actually matters.

The Danger of Declinism

Let's talk about what happens when we're convinced everything is getting worse, even when it's not.

First, it creates *learned helplessness*. If things are inevitably declining no matter what anyone does, why bother doing anything? Your actions don't matter because the trajectory is fixed. This is a self-fulfilling prophecy: when enough people believe action is futile, they stop taking action, which makes things worse, which confirms their belief that things are inevitably getting worse.

Second, it makes us *vulnerable to authoritarian promises*. Throughout history, demagogues have risen to power by convincing people that everything is falling apart and only they can restore a mythical golden age. "Make [Country] Great Again" only works as a slogan if people believe greatness has been lost. Declinism is the psychological foundation of authoritarianism.

Third, it *steals joy and presence*. If you're convinced the world is ending, you can't fully engage with or appreciate your actual life. Every good moment is overshadowed by the sense that it's all temporary, all doomed. You're so busy mourning the future that you miss the present.

Fourth, it makes us *dismissive of real progress and the people who created it*. When someone says "global poverty has declined dramatically," and your response is "yeah, but it shouldn't exist at all," you're implicitly dismissing the extraordinary work of millions of people who dedicated their lives to making that progress happen. Your inability to acknowledge improvement isn't sophisticated analysis. It's ingratitude dressed up as moral clarity.

And finally, declinism *disconnects us from reality*. If your worldview requires you to ignore or explain away positive data, you're not being realistic, you're being ideological. You've decided on a narrative (everything is getting worse) and you're contorting reality to fit that narrative rather than adjusting your narrative to fit reality.

I spent years doing this. Every piece of positive news was immediately reframed: "Sure, poverty is down, but that's just because of how they measure it." "Violence has decreased, but it's probably about to spike again." "People are living longer, but is longer life in this world really a good thing?"

I was so committed to my declinist narrative that I was actively fighting against good news. And I genuinely believed this made me more enlightened, more aware, more realistic than the naive optimists who didn't understand how bad things really were.

It didn't. It just made me miserable and ineffective.

Progress You've Never Heard About

Let me share some recent developments that probably didn't make your doom-scroll feed.

In the past decade, solar and wind energy have become cheaper than fossil fuels in most of the world. The cost of solar panels has dropped 90% in ten years. Renewable energy is now economically competitive without subsidies, which means the transition away from fossil fuels is increasingly driven by market forces, not just regulation.

Deforestation in the Amazon, while still a serious concern, has declined significantly from its peak in the early 2000s due to satellite monitoring, enforcement, and economic incentives. Several countries that were net deforesters have become net reforesters.

Malaria deaths have been cut in half since 2000. A malaria vaccine has been developed and is being distributed. River blindness and lymphatic filariasis are on track for elimination in dozens of countries.

The hole in the ozone layer—remember when that was going to kill us all?—is healing and expected to fully recover by mid-century, because humanity actually came together and banned the chemicals causing the damage. We identified a global environmental problem and fixed it. Collectively. As a species.

Gene therapy has cured children with previously fatal genetic diseases. CRISPR technology is advancing treatments for sickle cell anemia and other conditions. mRNA vaccine technology, developed in record time for COVID-19, is now being adapted for cancer treatment and other diseases.

More countries have legalized same-sex marriage in the past fifteen years than in all of prior human history. Acceptance of LGBTQ+ people has increased dramatically in a single generation, a shift in social attitudes that would have seemed impossible fifty years ago.

Youth smoking rates have plummeted. Teen pregnancy has declined to historic lows. Drunk driving deaths have dropped significantly. These aren't small things. They represent millions of lives saved and improved.

Communities around the world are developing innovative solutions to local problems such as urban farming projects, community solar programs, mutual aid networks, creative housing solutions, mental health support systems, violence interruption programs. Most of these never make national news, but they're real, they're working, and they're replicable.

None of this means we can stop working on problems. But it does mean that work matters. Action gets results. Progress is possible.

Reframing Progress

Here's what I've learned: Progress is not inevitable. It's not automatic.

It doesn't happen without effort, struggle, setbacks, and sustained commitment.

But it is possible. And that changes everything.

When I believed things were inevitably getting worse, I felt powerless. A spectator to collapse. But when I recognized that things have gotten better because people worked to make them better, and that things can continue to get better if we continue that work, I became an agent instead of a victim.

This doesn't mean being naive about challenges. I'm not suggesting we ignore climate change or inequality or any other serious problem. I'm suggesting that we're more likely to effectively address those problems if we're not starting from a place of hopeless despair.

The people who actually solve problems don't spend their time convinced that everything is fucked. They see a specific problem, believe it can be addressed, and get to work addressing it. They're not paralyzed by the enormity of everything wrong. They're energized by the possibility of making something better.

That's not toxic positivity. That's practical optimism. It's seeing reality clearly, both the challenges and the proven fact that humans can rise to meet challenges. And then choosing engagement over despair.

Progress isn't about everything being perfect. It's about things being better than they were, while acknowledging they could be better still. It's about trajectory, not destination.

And here's the kicker: Recognizing progress isn't the end of the work. It's the beginning. It's what gives us the energy, hope, and evidence-based confidence to tackle the next challenge.

You can't build a better world if you don't believe a better world is possible. And you can't believe a better world is possible if you can't see that we've already built one. Yes, it's imperfect, incomplete, but measurably better than what came before.

So yes, we face serious challenges. Some are new, some are persistent. They require urgent attention and sustained effort. But we've faced serious challenges before, and we've made progress on many of them. Not through despair and doom-saying, but through recognizing problems, believing solutions are possible, and doing the hard work to create them.

That's the truth about progress. It's not guaranteed. But it's also not impossible.

And that's all you need to get started.

4

Reclaiming Your Attention

I used to be a journalist, which means I was professionally trained in the art of consuming and producing information at an inhuman pace. Breaking news, developing stories, constant updates, multiple deadlines, endless feeds of content to monitor, digest, and respond to. My job was literally to pay attention to everything, all the damn time.

I was good at it. I could track six different stories simultaneously, scan dozens of sources in minutes, and maintain awareness of breaking developments across multiple platforms. I felt plugged into the pulse of the world. Informed. Alert. Essential. Alive.

I was also, it turns out, completely fucking miserable. I've made it back from the edge, and so can you!

The thing they don't tell you in journalism school, or maybe they do and nobody believes it until they experience it themselves, is that constant information consumption doesn't make you more informed. It makes you more anxious, more scattered, more reactive, and less capable of the deep thinking required to actually understand anything.

I would start my day checking Twitter before I got out of bed (sound familiar?). Then email. Then news sites. Then Slack. Then back to Twitter. By the time I actually started "working," I'd already processed hundreds of pieces of information, none of which I could recall fifteen minutes later. My attention was shattered into a thousand pieces before my day even began.

I told myself this was necessary. I was a journalist. Staying informed was my job. But here's what I've learned since leaving that world. The problem wasn't being a journalist. The problem was confusing attention with awareness, consumption with comprehension, and constant connectivity with actual understanding.

Your attention is being stolen from you, systematically and deliberately, by some of the most sophisticated behavioral engineers in human history. And unlike me, you don't even have the excuse of it being your job.

It's time to take it back.

The Attention Economy (And Why You're the Product)

Let's start with an uncomfortable truth. If you're not paying for a product, you are the product.

Social media platforms, news websites, apps, streaming services, they're all competing in what's called the "attention economy." Their business model is simple: capture your attention, hold it as long as possible, and sell that attention to advertisers. The longer you scroll, the more ads you see, the more money they make.

This means that every design choice, every algorithm tweak, every notification strategy is optimized for one thing: keeping you engaged. Not informed. Not happy. Not enriched. Just engaged.

They employ teams of psychologists, neuroscientists, and behavioral economists whose entire job is to make their platforms as addictive as possible. Variable reward schedules (like slot machines), infinite scroll, autoplay, carefully timed notifications, content algorithms learn your triggers. All of it is deliberately engineered to hijack your attention and make it nearly impossible to look away.

And it works. The average person checks their phone 96 times per day. Once every ten minutes! We spend over two hours per day on social media. We're interrupted by notifications every few minutes. Our attention span has shortened dramatically. Our capacity for sustained focus has atrophied.

This isn't an accident. It's the intended outcome of billions of dollars invested in making sure you can't stop scrolling.

When I was a journalist, I convinced myself I was different. I wasn't mindlessly scrolling. I was *working dammit!* I wasn't addicted. I was *professional!* But the truth is, my professional obligation to stay connected had trained me into patterns that persisted long after I logged off for the day. I had rewired my brain for distraction and called it expertise.

The first step in reclaiming your attention is recognizing that you're not weak-willed or undisciplined. You're up against some of the most sophisticated manipulation technology ever created, designed specifically to exploit your psychological vulnerabilities. Of course you're struggling.

But that doesn't mean you're powerless.

The Attention Audit: Where Does It Actually Go?

Before you can reclaim your attention, you need to understand where it's currently going. And I'm willing to bet your perception of how you spend your attention doesn't match reality.

Here's your first assignment: Track your attention for three days. Not what you think you're doing, but what you're actually doing.

Use your phone's screen time settings. Install a browser extension that tracks website visits. Keep a log. Be honest. Don't change your behavior yet. Just observe it.

At the end of three days, look at the data and ask yourself:

How much time did I spend consuming information versus creating something, connecting with someone, or taking action?
Most people discover they're spending 90% of their time consuming

and 10% creating or connecting. That ratio is backwards.

How much of my consumption was intentional versus reflexive? Did you deliberately decide to check the news, or did you just find yourself there? Did you choose to open social media, or did your thumb navigate there on autopilot?

How did I feel before and after each consumption session? Track this honestly. Did checking Twitter make you more informed and energized, or more anxious and depleted? Did reading the news help you understand something important, or just leave you angry and helpless?

What percentage of what I consumed do I actually remember? If you can't recall or summarize most of what you consumed yesterday, you weren't really taking in information. You were just exposing yourself to stimulation.

When did I lose time? Most people discover they have these black holes where they meant to "quickly check something" and emerged thirty minutes later having consumed dozens of pieces of content they didn't intend to see and can't remember.

When I did this exercise after leaving journalism, I was stunned. I thought I spent maybe an hour a day on Twitter. The data showed it was closer to three. I believed I was being selective about what I read. The logs showed I was compulsively checking the same sites over and over, often within minutes of my last visit, just in case something new had appeared.

I was spending enormous amounts of attention without any conscious decision to do so. My attention had become something that happened to me rather than something I controlled.

Sound familiar?

The Hidden Costs of Constant Connectivity

Let's talk about what all this scattered attention is actually costing you.

Fragmented focus means you never sink into deep work or deep presence. You're perpetually surface-level, skimming across the top of everything without fully engaging with anything. Studies show it takes an average of 23 minutes to fully regain focus after an interruption. If you're getting interrupted (or interrupting yourself) every ten minutes, you're never actually focused. You're living in a permanent state of semi-attention.

Decision fatigue accumulates throughout the day. Every notification, every headline, every bit of information you encounter requires micro-decisions: Read this? Skip it? Reply? Share? Care about this? Each tiny decision depletes your cognitive resources, leaving you exhausted even though you haven't actually accomplished anything significant.

Chronic stress from constant connectivity keeps your nervous system activated. Your body doesn't know the difference between a stressful headline and an actual threat to your safety. Every anxiety-inducing piece of content triggers a stress response: cortisol release, elevated heart rate, shallow breathing. Do that dozens of times a day, every day, and you're bathing your body in stress hormones even though you're just sitting on your couch scrolling.

Erosion of presence means you're not actually in your own life. You're at dinner with friends but mentally you're on Twitter. You're playing with your kids but part of your attention is on email. You're having a conversation but you're also watching a notification icon out of the corner of your eye. You're technically present but experientially absent.

Loss of deep thinking capacity. This is the one that terrified me most when I recognized it in myself. I used to be able to read long books, follow complex arguments, think through difficult problems. After years of constant information snacking, I found my brain rebelling against anything that required sustained attention. I was skimming everything, comprehending nothing deeply. My thoughts had become as fragmented as my attention.

The scariest part? This all felt normal. I had adapted to a state of chronic distraction and convinced myself it was just how modern life worked.

Attentional Nutrition: You Are What You Consume

You know how they say "you are what you eat"? The same is true for information consumption. You become what you repeatedly expose yourself to.

If you consume outrage all day, you become outraged. If you consume anxiety, you become anxious. If you consume shallow content, your thinking becomes shallow. If you consume contradictory fragments of information without context, your understanding of reality becomes fragmented and confused.

Think of your attention like nutrition. There's information junk food: designed for maximum palatability and addictiveness but with minimal nutritional value. Outrage porn, hot takes, celebrity gossip, algorithmic rage bait! It's engineered to be consumed, not to nourish you.

There's information fast food: convenient, ubiquitous, not terrible in moderation but deeply unhealthy as a primary diet. Headlines, tweets, short news clips, content optimized for shareability rather than accuracy or depth.

And then there's information whole food: long-form journalism, books, primary sources, in-depth analysis, genuine conversation. Harder to consume, requires more effort to digest, but actually nourishes your understanding.

Most of us are living on an information diet of almost pure junk and fast food. And then we wonder why our thinking feels malnourished, why we're mentally bloated but intellectually starving, why we consume constantly but never feel satisfied.

As a journalist, I thought I was eating information vegetables because I was consuming "news." But most news, especially breaking news and social media news, is closer to junk food than whole food. It's optimized for quick hits and emotional reactions, not deep understanding. Real comprehension requires time, context, and sustained attention. You can't understand complex issues through headlines any more than you can get adequate nutrition from energy drinks.

Practical Strategies for Reclaiming Your Attention

Okay, enough diagnosis. Let's talk about solutions.

Establish designated information times. Instead of grazing on news all day, set specific times when you'll catch up: maybe 20 minutes in the morning and 20 minutes in the evening. Outside those windows, news is closed. This isn't ignorance. It's boundaries. The world will not collapse if you're not monitoring it every hour.

Curate ruthlessly. Unfollow, unfriend, unsubscribe, mute, and block without guilt. Your social media feeds should serve you, not stress you. If an account consistently makes you feel worse, remove it. Yes, even if it's important issues. You can care about important issues without subjecting yourself to an algorithmically optimized rage stream about them.

Use technology to limit technology. Browser extensions like "Freedom," "StayFocusd," or "News Feed Eradicator" can block or limit access to time-wasting sites. Put social media apps in a folder on your phone's third screen. Turn off all non-essential notifications! And be honest about what's actually essential. (Hint: almost nothing is.)

Create phone-free zones. Make your bedroom a phone-free zone. No devices for the first hour after waking up or the last hour before sleep. No phones at meals. No phones during conversations with actual humans in the actual room. This will feel impossible at first. Do it anyway.

Distinguish between passive consumption and active engage-

ment. Lurking on social media, scrolling without posting or commenting, is consistently linked to increased depression and anxiety. If you're going to be online, actually engage. Have real conversations, contribute meaningfully, connect with specific people. Otherwise, close the app.

Read long-form instead of headlines. When you see a headline that triggers strong emotion, resist the urge to immediately react. Find the full article. Better yet, find multiple articles from different sources. Best yet, find the primary source. Most outrage evaporates when you actually understand the full context.

Seek out solution-focused journalism. There are outlets dedicated to covering not just problems but solutions: what's working, what's improving, what people are doing about challenges. This isn't ignoring difficulty. It's balancing awareness of problems with awareness of responses.

Build direct connections with causes you care about. Instead of consuming endless content about issues that matter to you, find one or two organizations working on those issues and engage directly. Volunteer. Donate. Attend meetings. Take action. This converts passive consumption into active contribution and dramatically reduces anxiety while increasing efficacy.

Practice "information intermittent fasting." Take regular breaks from all news and social media. Start with 24 hours. Then try a weekend. Work up to a full week. Notice what happens. Most people discover that the world continues without their constant monitoring, and they return feeling clearer and more energized rather than catastrophically uninformed.

FOMO and the Myth of Staying Informed

Let's address the anxiety I know is rising as you read these suggestions: "But what if I miss something important?"

Here's the truth: You're already missing most things. The amount of information generated every day is incomprehensibly vast. You could spend every waking moment consuming information and still miss 99.9999% of what's happening in the world. You're not staying informed that way. You're just sampling a tiny, algorithmically curated, emotionally manipulated slice of reality and convincing yourself it's comprehensive awareness.

And here's the other truth. Most "breaking news" isn't news you need to know right now. It's news that news organizations need you to pay attention to right now so they can sell ads or subscriptions. The handful of things that genuinely require immediate awareness such as a natural disaster in your area or a genuine emergency affecting people you know will reach you. Trust me. You will not miss the actual emergency because you weren't on X.

What you will miss by constantly consuming "news" is your actual life. The conversation with your partner. The sunset. The creative idea that needed quiet space to emerge. The rest your body needs. The deep work that requires focus. The presence with your own experience.

I used to believe that being a good journalist, and then a good citizen, required constant awareness of everything happening everywhere. It doesn't. It requires understanding the things you can actually influence or need to respond to, and accepting that you can't and do not need to monitor every crisis on the planet in real-time.

Constant awareness doesn't help anyone. It just leaves you too depleted to help anyone.

The 30-Day Attention Reset Challenge

Alright, here's your homework. Thirty days to rebuild your relationship with your attention. You don't have to do all of these. Just pick the ones that address your biggest attention leaks.

Week 1: Awareness

- Track your screen time and site visits daily
- Note how you feel before and after each major consumption session

- Identify your trigger moments (when you reflexively reach for your phone)
- No judgment, just observation

Week 2: Boundaries

- Set designated news times (twice a day maximum, 20 minutes each)
- Turn off all non-essential notifications
- Establish one phone-free zone in your life
- Delete or hide social media apps from your phone (you can still access via browser)

Week 3: Curation

- Unfollow/mute anyone who consistently makes you feel worse
- Subscribe to one long-form, solution-focused publication
- Find one organization working on an issue you care about and sign up for their newsletter
- Block or limit your three most time-wasting websites

Week 4: Integration

- Practice one full 24-hour information fast
- Start a practice of reading one long-form article per day
- Engage actively (comment, discuss, contribute) rather than passively consuming
- Before opening a social media or news app, ask: "What am I looking for right now?"

At the end of thirty days, do another attention audit. Track not just time but quality. Are you less anxious? More focused? Sleeping better?

Feeling more present? More capable of deep work?

I did this after I left journalism, and the results were dramatic. My anxiety decreased. My sleep improved. My capacity for sustained focus returned. I had more energy for creative work. My relationships deepened because I was actually present in conversations.

And here's the surprising part! I didn't feel less informed. I felt more informed, because the information I was consuming, I was actually comprehending and retaining. I was replacing quantity with quality, fragments with coherence, reactivity with intention.

Taking Back What's Yours

Your attention is the most valuable resource you have. It's more valuable than your money, because it's how you spend your actual life. Every moment of attention is a moment of your existence. Where your attention goes, your life goes.

And right now, your attention is being stolen, systematically and deliberately, by entities that profit from your distraction and depletion.

This isn't about being a Luddite or disconnecting from the world. It's about being intentional instead of reactive. It's about choosing what deserves your attention instead of letting algorithms choose for you. It's about consuming information that nourishes your understanding instead of junk food that just makes you anxious.

You can be informed without being consumed. You can be aware without being obsessed. You can care about the world without drowning in its every crisis.

But first, you have to take your attention back. It's yours. Reclaim it.

5

The Power of Realistic Optimism

There's a specific type of person who makes me immediately suspicious, and if you've spent any time on the internet, you know the type too. They're the relentlessly upbeat motivational guru who insists that everything happens for a reason, that the universe has a plan, and that you can manifest your dreams through positive thinking alone.

You know what I'm talking about. The "good vibes only" crowd. The people who respond to genuine problems with "just think positive!" The ones who treat optimism like a moral obligation and any acknowledgment of difficulty as a character flaw.

These people are exhausting. And they're giving optimism a bad name.

Because here's the thing about toxic positivity. The denial of difficulty and the insistence on positive thinking regardless of circumstances is not optimism. It's delusion with a smile. And it's just as disconnected from reality as fatalistic pessimism, except it forces you to pretend everything's fine while Rome burns.

Real optimism is something entirely different. It's not about denying reality but seeing reality clearly and still maintaining agency. It's not about believing everything will magically work out either. It's about believing your efforts matter and that positive outcomes are possible.

The difference between toxic positivity and realistic optimism is the difference between "everything is fine!" and "things are hard, and we can handle hard things."

One denies truth. The other confronts it with hope.

Tragic Optimism: Hope in the Face of Reality

Tragic optimism is the capacity to maintain hope and find meaning even in the face of unavoidable suffering. It's not pretending suffering doesn't exist or isn't real. It's not toxic positivity saying "everything happens for a reason" or "this will make you stronger." It's the clear-eyed recognition that life includes genuine tragedy. And that we can still choose our response to that tragedy.

This isn't naive. It's possibly the most sophisticated psychological insight available to us: that our circumstances don't determine our experience. Our response to those circumstances does.

Notice what this is not saying. It's not saying "just think positive and your problems will disappear." It's saying that even when problems won't disappear, you still have agency over how you engage with them. You can choose despair or you can choose meaning. You can choose paralysis or you can choose action. You can choose to be destroyed by difficulty or to find purpose in confronting it.

This is what realistic optimism looks like when facing genuine hardship. Not denial, not toxic positivity, but the recognition that even in the worst circumstances, we retain the freedom to choose our relationship to those circumstances.

The Science of Optimism

Your explanatory style is how you explain events to yourself, particularly negative events. Pessimists tend to explain bad events as permanent ("things will always be this bad"), pervasive ("this ruins everything"), and personal ("it's my fault"). Optimists explain the same events as temporary ("this is a current challenge"), specific ("this affects this one area"), and external or changeable ("circumstances contributed, and circumstances can change").

Here's what's fascinating: this explanatory style affects everything. Seligman's research shows that optimists have better mental health, stronger immune systems, more successful relationships, and higher achievement in school and work. Not because optimists don't face difficulties, they face the same difficulties as everyone else. But their explanatory style keeps them engaged and active rather than hopeless and passive.

And crucially, pessimists aren't more accurate. Studies consistently show that pessimists overestimate how bad things are and how long problems will last. They think their negative predictions are realistic, but they're actually just negative. Meanwhile, optimists, while sometimes too rosy about timing, are generally more accurate about eventual outcomes.

The pessimist says, "I tried and failed, which proves I can't do it, so I should give up." The optimist says, "I tried and failed, which gives me information about what doesn't work, so I can try differently." Same event, radically different interpretation, completely different outcome.

Why Pessimism Feels Smart

If optimism is more accurate, more effective, and better for your health, why does pessimism feel so much more intelligent?

Because in our culture, cynicism is coded as sophistication. The person who points out problems sounds smart. The person who suggests solutions sounds naive. The critic sounds intellectual. The builder sounds simplistic.

We've created a weird status hierarchy where being negative about everything signals that you're informed, aware, and too smart to be fooled. Meanwhile, being hopeful signals that you're either ignorant of how bad things are or intellectually unsophisticated enough to believe they could improve.

This is, to put it bluntly, completely backwards.

Pessimism isn't realism. It's a cognitive bias (remember negativity bias from Chapter 2?). And cynicism isn't wisdom but it's often intellectual laziness. It's much easier to tear things down than to build them up. It's much easier to explain why something won't work than to figure out how to make it work. It's much easier to maintain detached ironic distance than to earnestly engage with actually solving problems.

The pessimist gets to feel smart while doing nothing. The optimist has to put in the work and risk looking foolish. Guess which one our culture rewards in conversation, even as optimists are out building the actual future?

Here's the uncomfortable truth: pessimists often feel more intelligent, but optimists are generally more effective. Pessimism sounds sophisticated but leads to paralysis. Optimism might sound naive but drives action. And action is what actually changes things.

Frameworks for Realistic Optimism

So how do you actually cultivate this? How do you acknowledge reality without drowning in despair? Here are practical frameworks:

Acknowledge current reality, then shift to agency. Start by stating the truth clearly: "This situation is genuinely difficult." Then add: "And here's what I can influence." This isn't denying the difficulty. It's refusing to let difficulty be the end of the sentence.

Identify what's in your control. You can't control the economy, politics, or other people. You can control your actions, reactions, effort, and choices about where to focus energy. Realistic optimism focuses on the latter while acknowledging the former exists.

Focus on next steps, not final outcomes. You don't have to solve everything. You don't have to have it all figured out. You just need to identify the next right action. Realistic optimism asks: "What's one thing I can do today?" not "How do I fix everything forever?"

Find meaning in struggle. Suffering becomes unbearable when it feels meaningless, but the same suffering becomes endurable when we find purpose in it. What can this difficulty teach you? Who are you becoming through facing it? What matters in how you respond?

Practice "yes, and" thinking instead of "yes, but." The pessimist says: "Yes, that might work, but here are seventeen reasons it will fail." The realistic optimist says: "Yes, that might work, and here's what we'd need to address to increase the chances." Same awareness of challenges, radically different orientation toward action.

Building Self-Efficacy

Self-efficacy is the belief in your capacity to influence outcomes. This isn't generic self-esteem or confidence but domain-specific belief that your actions can produce desired results.

Self-efficacy is built through four main sources:

Mastery experiences: Actually succeeding at things, even small things. Each time you set a goal and achieve it, you strengthen your belief that you can influence outcomes. Start small. Stack up wins.

Vicarious experiences: Seeing people similar to you succeed. This is why representation matters and why surrounding yourself with people who are actively making things better (rather than just complaining) is crucial.

Social persuasion: Having others believe in your capacity. Find people who see your potential and reflect it back to you. Avoid people who constantly tell you why things won't work.

Physiological states: Managing your stress and energy so you approach challenges from a state of capability rather than depletion. (This is why self-care isn't selfish but strategic.)

Realistic optimism grows from self-efficacy. When you have evidence, from your own experience and others', that action produces results, you can maintain optimism even when facing difficulty because you know you're not helpless.

The Strategic Advantage of Optimism

Here's the bottom line. Realistic optimism isn't just emotionally healthier but it's strategically smarter.

Pessimism makes you scan for threats and problems, which can be useful for risk assessment but terrible for solution-finding. Your brain in pessimistic mode is defensive, reactive, and narrow in its thinking.

Optimism makes you scan for opportunities and possibilities. Your brain in optimistic mode is creative, proactive, and expansive in its thinking. You see more options, generate more solutions, and take more action.

Every innovation, every social movement, every positive change in human history required someone to believe change was possible despite evidence that it was difficult. Pessimists said it wouldn't work. Optimists made it work anyway.

This doesn't mean being naive about obstacles. It means maintaining the mental flexibility and creative energy required to navigate obstacles. It means staying engaged instead of giving up.

The realistic optimist says: "This is hard, and I'm going to try anyway. The outcome isn't certain, but effort improves the odds. I might fail, and that failure will give me information for the next attempt. The future isn't predetermined. My actions influence it."

That's not delusion. That's accurate assessment of how change actually happens.

You can see reality clearly and still maintain hope. You can acknowledge difficulty and still take action. You can confront brutal facts and still believe in eventual triumph.

That's the power of realistic optimism. Not pretending everything is fine. Knowing it's hard, and choosing to engage anyway.

Because you're not fucked. The situation might be difficult. The odds might be uncertain. The outcome might be unknown.

But you still have agency. Your efforts still matter. Positive outcomes are still possible.

And that's all you need to get started.

6

Your Sphere of Influence

I once had a panic attack in the cereal aisle.

Not because I was overwhelmed by choice, though there were approximately four hundred varieties of breakfast options brightly assaulting my senses. But because I was standing there, staring at boxes of corn flakes, while simultaneously carrying the weight of climate change, three active war zones, a political crisis, economic inequality, a refugee crisis, the erosion of democracy, and the fact that I hadn't called my mother in two weeks. I was being crushed right on my chest. It felt that way.

The thought that broke me was: "I should probably buy the organic cereal because of pesticides and also I'm a terrible person for thinking about cereal when children are dying."

My partner found me frozen in place, tears streaming down my face, unable to choose between Cheerios and the void.

This is what happens when you're chronically unable to distinguish between things you're responsible for and things you're just aware of. When your hyperconnected brain treats every problem you encounter, from the personal to the planetary, as your personal burden to carry.

You end up sobbing in the cereal aisle while your nervous system screams that you're simultaneously doing too much and not nearly enough.

The Tyranny of Infinite Responsibility

Here's a truth that our hyperconnected age has made unbearably acute: you cannot be responsible for everything you're aware of.

But try telling that to your guilt complex.

The internet has given us unprecedented access to suffering. At any moment, you can scroll through genocides, natural disasters, injustices, crises, and tragedies from every corner of the planet. You can read first-person accounts of suffering. You can watch videos. You can see the names and faces of people in pain.

And somewhere in your psyche, a voice whispers: "You know about this. You should do something. If you don't do something, you're complicit. You're part of the problem."

This voice is trying to make you a good person. But it's actually making you a paralyzed person.

Because here's what that voice doesn't account for: the human nervous system did not evolve to carry awareness of global suffering. We evolved in small tribes where we knew maybe 150 people, and the suffering we encountered was suffering we could directly impact. You saw someone hungry, you shared food. You saw someone in danger, you helped.

Now you're aware of millions of people suffering, and you cannot help most of them. You can feel for them, yes. You can care about them, absolutely. But you cannot fix their problems. And the gap between your awareness and your capacity creates a psychological state that's essentially unbearable.

So you end up with what I call "omnipresent guilt." That's the constant background hum of feeling like you should be doing more, caring more, giving more, while simultaneously feeling like whatever you do is inadequate.

And here's the cruelest part: this guilt doesn't motivate effective action. It motivates paralysis, burnout, and breakdowns in cereal aisles.

Three Circles: Control, Influence, and Concern

Think of your relationship to the world's problems as three concentric circles.

The innermost circle is your circle of control. This is what you can directly determine through your choices and actions: your behaviors, reactions, habits, how you spend your time and money, how you treat people in your life, what you say, how you show up. This circle is smaller than you probably wish it was, but it's real and it's yours.

The middle circle is your circle of influence. This is what you can affect but not fully control: your immediate relationships, your workplace culture, your local community, perhaps local politics or organizations you're part of. You can't determine outcomes here, but your actions genuinely matter and create ripples.

The outer circle is your circle of concern. This is everything you care about but cannot directly control or significantly influence: global politics, international conflicts, macro-economic trends, climate systems, what strangers do, what happened in the past, what might happen in the future. This circle is enormous and growing every time you open the news or scroll through social media.

Here's the problem: most of us are living in our circle of concern.

We spend our mental and emotional energy obsessing over things we cannot control, feeling responsible for things we cannot influence, and carrying guilt about not solving problems we have no direct ability to solve. Meanwhile, our actual circles of control and influence, the places where we could make real differences, get neglected because we're too depleted from trying to carry the world.

It's like standing in your own house, which needs cleaning, while staring out the window at a neighbor's house across town that's on fire, feeling guilty that you're not over there with a bucket. Meanwhile, your house remains uncleaned, and the fire department, which can actually help, is already on the way.

The Psychological Toll of Misplaced Responsibility

Living primarily in your circle of concern creates specific forms of suffering:

Chronic helplessness. When you focus on what you cannot control, you train your brain in helplessness. Every day reinforces the message: "I'm aware of terrible things and I can't do anything about them." This learned helplessness spreads, eventually making you feel powerless even in areas where you do have agency.

Decision paralysis. If every choice has global implications (your cereal purchase affects pesticide use, which affects pollinators, which affects ecosystems, which affects climate), every decision becomes impossibly weighted. You freeze, overwhelmed by the complexity of consequences you can't fully trace or control.

Performative guilt. You feel bad about things, post about feeling bad, maybe make small gestures to alleviate the bad feelings, but don't actually change anything significant. The guilt becomes its own kind of comfort. At least you feel appropriately terrible about the state of the world, even if that feeling doesn't translate to effective action.

Resentment and burnout. You can't sustain caring about everything at maximum intensity. Eventually, you either shut down completely or develop a bitter cynicism toward causes, activism, and even your own values. You burn out not from doing too much but from caring about too much while doing too little that actually matters.

Neglect of your actual life. While you're consuming content about global crises, your relationships languish. Your local community, a place where you could actually contribute, doesn't get your energy. Your mental health deteriorates. You become less capable of helping anyone, including yourself.

Right-Sizing Your Responsibility

Here's the liberating truth that might also make you uncomfortable: being aware of a problem does not make it your personal responsibility to fix.

You can know about distant suffering without carrying it constantly. You can care about global issues without making them your primary focus. You can acknowledge injustice without making yourself accountable for correcting all of it.

This isn't apathy. This is sustainability.

Think of it like the oxygen mask principle on airplanes: secure your own mask before helping others. Not because you don't care about others, but because you can't help anyone if you've passed out from lack of oxygen.

Your circles of control and influence are your oxygen masks. These are where you can actually make a difference, where your actions have clear impacts, where you can see results and build on them. Master these before you exhaust yourself trying to control the uncontrollable.

This means:

- Focus your energy on relationships you're actually in, not parasocial relationships with strangers online
- Engage with your actual neighborhood before trying to solve homelessness nationally
- Show up to local meetings before despairing about federal policy
- Have real conversations with people you know before arguing with strangers on the internet
- Build something tangible in your community before trying to change global systems

Does this mean ignoring global problems? No. It means recognizing that for most global problems, the most effective thing most of us can do is build strong, functional, compassionate communities locally. Systemic change requires systems, and systems are built from functioning parts. Be a functioning part.

Moral Residue and How to Process It

There's a concept from healthcare called "moral residue." That's the psychological weight that accumulates when you witness suffering you cannot prevent or fix. Nurses experience it when they have to provide inadequate care due to systemic constraints. It's the gap between what you believe should happen and what you can actually make happen.

In our hyperconnected age, we all carry moral residue. We see suffering we cannot directly address. We know about injustices we cannot personally correct. We're aware of problems that exceed our individual capacity to solve.

This residue is real and it's heavy. Denying it leads to burnout or cynicism. But drowning in it leads to paralysis.

Here's how to process it:

Acknowledge the limits of your capacity without self-blame. "I cannot solve this problem" is not a moral failing. It's a statement of fact. Your finite capacity is not evidence of inadequate caring.

Distinguish between awareness and action. You can be informed about issues without making them your primary focus. You can care without carrying. You can stay aware without staying consumed.

Find appropriate channels for the concerns that live in your outer circle. This might mean you donating to organizations that work on those issues, signing petitions, voting, or sharing resources. These are all forms of engagement that don't require you to personally solve problems beyond your scope.

Practice grief without guilt. It's okay to feel sad about suffering you cannot prevent. That sadness is appropriate. What's not necessary is the guilt that says you should be able to prevent it.

Return to your circles of influence. After acknowledging distant problems, actively redirect your energy to where you can make real impact. This isn't ignoring the distant but honoring what you can actually do.

Where You Have More Influence Than You Think

Here's what's easy to miss while obsessing over things you can't control: you probably have more influence than you realize in your immediate sphere.

In your relationships, you can: initiate difficult conversations, show up consistently, offer specific help, be trustworthy, apologize when you're wrong, celebrate people's wins, witness their struggles.

In your workplace, you can mentor someone, improve one process, speak up about one problem, start one conversation, build one collaboration, make someone's day slightly better.

In your community, you can introduce neighbors to each other, organize one gathering, volunteer for one thing, support one local business, show up to one meeting, pick up trash on one street.

These actions might sound small compared to solving climate change or ending war. But here's what decades of community organizing and social movement research shows: large-scale change is built from accumulated small-scale actions. Movements aren't made by isolated heroes fixing everything. They're made by thousands of people doing their part in their sphere.

Your small sphere isn't a cop-out. It's the foundation.

The Ripple Effect

When you act effectively in your circle of influence, ripples extend beyond it in ways you cannot control or predict.

You help one person, who feels less alone, who then helps someone else. You improve one process at work, which gets noticed and replicated. You start one conversation that shifts one perspective that changes one vote that influences one policy. You cannot trace or control these ripples, but they're real.

This is how change actually works. Not through individual heroes saving the world, but through networks of people making things slightly better in their domains, with those improvements cascading and compounding.

But you never see those ripples if you're too depleted from trying to boil the ocean to actually heat your own cup of water.

The Guilt of Focusing Locally

"But how can I worry about my community garden when there are wars and famines?"

This question contains a false choice. It implies that caring about local things means not caring about global things. But that's not how it works.

You can care about war and famine by staying informed, supporting relevant organizations, voting for leaders with sane foreign policies, raising awareness when appropriate, and then returning to your actual life and your actual community where your actual hands can do actual work.

The community garden isn't a distraction from solving global problems. It's you doing your part: building local food systems, creating green space, fostering community connection, teaching skills, providing beauty and nourishment. These things matter. They're not less important because they're local but they're more effective because they're local.

You don't have to choose between caring globally and acting locally. You can care globally and act locally because that's actually how you contribute most effectively.

You Don't Have to Fix Everything

Here's your permission slip: You don't have to fix everything. You don't have to solve every problem you're aware of. You don't have to carry guilt for having limits.

You just have to do your part.

And "your part" looks like: showing up in your own life, tending your relationships, contributing to your community, acting in alignment with your values in your daily choices, and using your specific skills and resources in your specific context to make things slightly better where you are.

That's it. That's enough.

Not because global problems don't matter, but because you're not capable of solving them all yourself and pretending you should be is destroying you without helping anyone.

Focus your energy where you have genuine influence. Stop trying to control what you can't. Let go of responsibility for problems beyond your scope without letting go of your values.

This isn't giving up. This is getting strategic. This is recognizing that sustainable engagement requires boundaries, and effective action requires focus.

You're not responsible for fixing the world. You're responsible for your part of it.

And when enough of us actually tend our parts instead of drowning in guilt about all the parts we can't tend, that's when things actually change.

7

Building Your Resilience Toolkit

Resilience has become one of those buzzwords that gets thrown around so much it's practically meaningless. Corporate seminars teach resilience so employees can tolerate terrible working conditions. Self-help gurus sell resilience as some kind of superpower that makes you impervious to pain. Politicians praise resilience in communities while cutting the services those communities need.

So let's be clear about what resilience actually is. It's not about being unbreakable. It's not about never struggling. It's not about powering through everything with a smile and a can-do attitude.

Resilience is the capacity to get knocked down and get back up. To face difficulty without being permanently destroyed by it. To bend without breaking, or to break and then heal. It's not invulnerability, instead it's flexibility, recovery, and sustained capacity to keep engaging with life even when life is hard.

And here's what nobody tells you: resilience isn't built through exotic practices or expensive programs. It's built through unglamorous basics that most of us are neglecting because we're too busy looking for shortcuts.

The Boring Foundation: Sleep, Food, Movement, Connection

I know you want me to tell you about some advanced psycholog-ical technique or ancient wisdom practice that will transform your resilience overnight. But I'm going to start with something far less sexy: are you sleeping enough?

No, seriously. When was the last time you got seven to eight hours of quality sleep consistently for a week?

Because here's the thing: you cannot build resilience on a foundation of sleep deprivation. Your brain literally cannot regulate emotions effectively without adequate sleep. Your body cannot manage stress without rest. You cannot make good decisions, maintain perspective, or access your coping skills when you're chronically exhausted.

Sleep is not a luxury you'll get to once you've solved all your problems. Sleep is the foundation that gives you the capacity to address problems in the first place.

Same with nutrition. You don't need a perfect diet or expensive superfoods. You need regular meals with actual nutrients. Your brain runs on glucose. Your neurotransmitters are built from the food you eat. When you're undernourished or running on coffee and anxiety, your resilience plummets.

Movement matters. Not because you need to look a certain way, but because your body is designed to move and processes stress through movement. Sitting still while cortisol floods your system is like revving your car engine while keeping it in park. You're generating energy with nowhere for it to go. Walk. Dance. Stretch. Move the stress through and out.

And social connection—actual connection with actual humans—is one of the most powerful predictors of resilience. Isolation makes everything harder. Community makes everything more bearable. This isn't soft psychology. It is hard biology. Humans are social animals. We literally regulate each other's nervous systems through connection.

I know these basics seem obvious to the point of insulting. But most people I talk to who are struggling with resilience are not doing these things consistently. They're looking for advanced solutions while ignoring the foundation. It's like trying to build a second story on a house with no first floor.

You want resilience? Start with sleep, food, movement, and connection. Everything else is secondary.

Stress Inoculation: Building Strength Through Challenge

Here's a counterintuitive truth about resilience: you don't build it by avoiding stress. You build it by facing manageable amounts of stress successfully.

This is called stress inoculation, and it works like a vaccine. You expose yourself to a small, controlled dose of the thing that challenges you, and your system develops capacity to handle bigger versions of it later.

Kids who are protected from every minor disappointment don't develop resilience. They become fragile. Adults who avoid all discomfort don't build strength but shrink their capacity. Meanwhile, people who regularly face and overcome challenges, even small ones, develop confidence in their ability to handle difficulty.

The key word here is "manageable." You're not throwing yourself into the deep end before you can swim. You're gradually increasing the difficulty as your capacity grows.

This might look like: having a difficult conversation you've been avoiding, trying something new where you might fail, setting a boundary with someone, taking on a project that stretches you, sitting with uncomfortable emotions instead of immediately distracting from them.

Each time you face something challenging and survive it, even if you don't handle it perfectly, you build evidence for yourself that you can handle hard things. This evidence accumulates into resilience.

Mindset: Threat vs. Challenge

How you frame difficulty matters enormously.

When you encounter a problem, your brain makes a rapid assessment: Is this a threat (something that will harm me that I can't handle) or a challenge (something difficult that I can potentially navigate)?

Threat mindset activates your stress response: cortisol floods your system, your thinking narrows, your body prepares for fight-or-flight, you focus on avoiding harm. This is useful when you're facing actual danger, but destructive when applied to most modern difficulties.

Challenge mindset activates your engagement response: you get an energy boost, your thinking becomes more creative, your body prepares for action, you focus on approaching the problem. You're still taking it seriously, but you're oriented toward solving it rather than just surviving it.

Same situation, radically different physiological and psychological response, completely different outcomes.

The shift is subtle but powerful. Instead of "This is going to destroy me," try "This is going to be hard, and I can handle hard things." Instead of "I can't do this," try "I can't do this yet, but I can learn." Instead of "Everything is falling apart," try "This specific thing is difficult right now."

You're not denying reality but you're simply framing it in a way that keeps you capable rather than paralyzed.

Practical Tools: Mindfulness, Reframing, Writing

Mindfulness has been oversold as some kind of spiritual enlightenment practice, but strip away the mysticism and it's just mental training. You're teaching your brain to stay with present experience instead of spiraling into anxiety about the future or rumination about the past.

Start simple: five minutes a day of just noticing your breath. When your mind wanders (it will, constantly), you notice and return to the breath. That's it. You're not trying to stop thoughts or achieve some blissed-out state. You're building the skill of noticing where your attention is and redirecting it intentionally.

This skill transfers to everything else. When you notice you're catastrophizing, you can redirect. When you notice you're ruminating, you can choose differently. Mindfulness isn't about feeling peaceful but about having more choice in where your attention goes.

Cognitive reframing is catching your automatic interpretations and questioning them. Your brain constantly narrates events ("This means I'm failing," "Everyone thinks I'm incompetent," "Things will never get better"). These narratives feel like facts but they're only interpretations. And they're often wildly inaccurate.

When you catch a destructive narrative, ask: What's the evidence for this? What's the evidence against it? What's an alternative interpretation? What would I tell a friend in this situation?

Expressive writing helps process difficult experiences. Twenty minutes of writing about what you're struggling with has been shown to improve both mental and physical health. You're getting the experience out of your head and onto paper where you can examine it more objectively. You don't need to show this writing to anyone.

The Role of Joy, Play, and Rest

Here's where resilience training goes wrong: we treat it like boot camp. All discipline, all grinding through difficulty, all serious preparation for hardship.

But joy, play, and rest aren't rewards you get after building resilience. They're nutrients that build resilience.

Joy isn't frivolous. It's restorative. Moments of genuine delight, beauty, humor, connection—these refill your reserves. If your life is all stress management with no actual enjoyment, you're running on empty.

Play isn't childish. It's essential. Doing things purely for enjoyment, without productivity or purpose, gives your nervous system permission to relax. Adults who never play become brittle. Creativity, spontaneity, and flexibility all come from a nervous system that knows it's safe to experiment and enjoy.

Rest isn't laziness. It's strategic. You cannot sustain effort without recovery. Athletes know this. Musicians know this. Everyone else seems to think they can run at maximum capacity indefinitely and then wonders why they burn out.

If you want resilience, you need to actively cultivate joy, play, and rest. It should be a regular practices.

Resilience Inequity: When the Playing Field Isn't Level

I need to address something that gets ignored in most resilience conversations: resilience is harder for some people than others due to structural factors completely outside their control.

Someone dealing with poverty has to be resilient just to meet basic needs. Someone facing discrimination has to be resilient against constant systemic barriers. Someone with trauma history has to work harder to regulate a nervous system that's been wired for hypervigilance.

Individual resilience practices are valuable for everyone, but they're not substitutes for addressing the conditions that make resilience necessary in the first place. When we only focus on individual resilience, we implicitly blame people for not handling situations that shouldn't exist.

Yes, build your personal resilience. And also recognize that some people are being asked to be resilient against circumstances that should change. Individual coping skills matter, but so does collective action to reduce the amount of resilience required to just exist.

Protocols for Acute and Chronic Stress

For acute stress (panic attack, crisis moment, overwhelming emotion):

Box breathing: Breathe in for 4 counts, hold for 4, out for 4, hold for 4. Repeat until your nervous system calms. This is physiology. Deep breathing activates your parasympathetic nervous system.

5-4-3-2-1 grounding: Name 5 things you can see, 4 you can touch, 3 you can hear, 2 you can smell, 1 you can taste. This pulls you out of panic and into present sensory reality.

Temperature change: Splash cold water on your face, hold ice, step outside. Sudden temperature change can interrupt a stress spiral.

For chronic stress (ongoing difficulty, sustained pressure):

Boundary setting: Identify what's depleting you and create limits. Say no more. Protect your energy like the finite resource it is.

Energy management: Track what drains you and what recharges you. Schedule recharging activities as non-negotiable appointments, not optional if-there's-time extras.

Sustainable routines: Build practices you can maintain even on bad days. A 5-minute practice you do consistently beats an hour-long practice you do once.

Your Personal Resilience Assessment

Take inventory of what you already have:

Resources: Who are your people? What practices already help? What skills have gotten you through past difficulties? What brings you joy or peace? What's in your control?

Gaps: Where are you depleted? What basics are you neglecting? What skills do you need to develop? Where do you need more support?

Action plan: Based on your gaps, what's one thing you can address this week? Just one thing. Build from there.

Resilience Is Collective

Final truth: resilience isn't just individual. We build it together.

You're more resilient when you're part of a community that shares resources, supports each other, celebrates together, and carries each other through hard times. Rugged individualism is a myth. Humans have always survived through cooperation.

Your resilience toolkit should include people you can call, communities you belong to, ways to give and receive support, shared practices and rituals.

You don't have to be strong alone. In fact, you can't be, at least not sustainably. Real resilience is built through connection, not isolation. So yes, work on your individual practices. Sleep enough. Move your body. Practice mindfulness. Manage your stress. But also: invest in relationships, show up for community, ask for help, offer help, build networks of mutual support.

That's how you build resilience that lasts. Not by becoming invulnerable, but by becoming connected, flexible, and capable of bending without breaking. Together.

8

The Gratitude Revolution

If you've spent any time on Instagram, you've seen gratitude performed. It's all perfectly filtered photos of sunrises with captions about being #blessed, influencers thanking the universe for their abundance, carefully curated lists of blessings that somehow always include "my amazing journey" and "this incredible community."

This version of gratitude makes me want to throw things.

Not because gratitude itself is bad. It's not. But because we've turned it into a performance, a brand, a way to signal spiritual enlightenment or positive vibes. We've made it shallow, aesthetic, and vaguely insulting to anyone dealing with actual hardship.

"Just be grateful!" people chirp at those struggling with depression, poverty, or trauma, as if gratitude is a magic spell that makes real problems disappear. As if the issue isn't the circumstances but your ungrateful attitude toward them.

So let me be clear. That performative, toxic-positivity, bypass-your-real-feelings version of gratitude can fuck right off.

But there's another kind of gratitude. It's private, unglamorous, often uncomfortable. That's genuinely revolutionary. Not because it makes problems disappear, but because it helps you maintain the emotional

74

resources to face them.

Let's reclaim gratitude from the motivational poster people and talk about what it actually does.

The Science: Your Brain on Gratitude

Here's what happens in your brain when you practice genuine gratitude regularly:

Your neural pathways literally rewire. fMRI studies show that gratitude practice increases activity in the medial prefrontal cortex (involved in decision-making and emotional regulation) and reduces activity in the amygdala (your brain's threat-detection center). Over time, this rewiring becomes your new baseline. Your brain becomes better at noticing positive things and less reactive to threats.

Your body chemistry changes. Gratitude practice increases serotonin and dopamine. Your brain's feel-good neurotransmitters. Not like a temporary high, but as a sustained shift in baseline neurochemistry. People who practice gratitude regularly show lower levels of cortisol (stress hormone) and inflammation markers.

Your physical health improves. Studies show people with regular gratitude practices have stronger immune systems, lower blood pressure, better sleep, and less chronic pain. This isn't woo-woo. It's measurable physiological change.

Your relationships strengthen. Expressing gratitude to others increases relationship satisfaction, encourages prosocial behavior, and creates positive feedback loops of mutual appreciation.

Your resilience increases. Grateful people recover from adversity faster and report higher life satisfaction even when facing genuine difficulties.

None of this is controversial. The research is robust and replicated. Gratitude practice works. The question is: why does it feel so fake and forced for so many people?

Why Gratitude Feels Impossible

Let me guess your resistance. Maybe it's one of these:

"Gratitude feels like toxic positivity." You're right to be suspicious of anyone who tells you to "just be grateful" while dismissing your real struggles. That's minimization. Real gratitude doesn't deny problems; it coexists with them.

"Life is genuinely hard right now, finding things to be grateful for feels forced." Yes. It will feel forced at first. That's because you've trained your brain to prioritize threats and problems (remember negativity bias?). Gratitude practice is retraining, and retraining always feels awkward initially.

"If I focus on good things, I'll become complacent about problems." This fear makes sense, but it's backwards. Research shows grateful people are actually *more* likely to take action on problems, not less. Because gratitude builds the emotional resources and energy needed for engagement. Burnout and despair don't motivate effective action. Hope and resilience do.

"It feels fake, like I'm lying to myself." If you're writing "I'm grateful for my amazing life" when your life feels like a dumpster fire, yeah, that's lying. But noticing "I'm grateful for this coffee" or "I'm grateful my friend texted" isn't lying. Those things are genuinely there. You're not making up positives; you're noticing ones that already exist but that you've been filtering out.

"Gratitude feels like settling or giving up." Gratitude isn't about lowering standards or accepting unacceptable situations. It's about maintaining perspective and emotional balance while you work to change what needs changing.

The resistance is real, and it's valid. What's not valid is letting that resistance keep you from a practice that measurably improves wellbeing.

Performative vs. Genuine Gratitude

Performative gratitude is for an audience. It's about signaling spiritual evolution, positive energy, or success. It's curated and aesthetic. It feels good to post but doesn't change your actual experience.

Genuine gratitude is private and messy. It's noticing the specific things, often small, often mundane, that sustain you. It's not for Instagram. It's not even necessarily about big things. It's "I'm grateful the sun came through my window this morning" or "I'm grateful I have clean water" or "I'm grateful my body is letting me feel this difficult emotion."

Genuine gratitude often coexists with difficulty. You can be grateful for your friend's support while also being angry about the situation that made support necessary. You can be grateful for healthcare while also furious about the healthcare system. You can be grateful for what works while still fighting to fix what doesn't.

This is what I call **complex gratitude**, which is holding appreciation and criticism simultaneously. Not either/or, but both/and.

Gratitude Practices That Actually Work

Forget the "list three things before bed" approach if it's not working for you. Here are alternatives:

Gratitude letters (undelivered). Think of someone who has positively impacted your life. Write them a detailed letter explaining specifically what they did and how it affected you. You don't have to send it—the act of writing it is what matters. This practice produces some of the most robust increases in wellbeing of any gratitude intervention.

Gratitude walks. Take a walk with the specific intention of noticing things to appreciate. Not big philosophical gratitudes, but specific sensory details: the color of that building, the smell of rain, the sound of birds, the feeling of your body moving. This combines movement (good for stress) with attention training (noticing what's working).

Savoring practice. When something genuinely good happens, even something small, pause and fully experience it for 30 seconds. Notice the details. Let yourself feel the pleasure. We tend to rush past positive experiences while dwelling on negative ones. Savoring rebalances that.

Obstacle gratitude. This is advanced practice, but it's powerful: identify something difficult you're facing and ask what it's teaching you or what strength it's building. Not "everything happens for a reason" toxic positivity, but genuine exploration of what you're learning through struggle. Sometimes the answer is just "I'm learning I can survive hard things." That counts.

Specificity over generalities. Instead of "I'm grateful for my family," try "I'm grateful my partner made coffee this morning" or "I'm grateful my kid told me about their day." Specific gratitudes feel more real and activate your brain more powerfully than vague ones.

Gratitude as Antidote to Comparison and Envy

Social media has weaponized comparison. Everyone else's highlight reel makes your regular life feel inadequate. Someone is always richer, more successful, more attractive, traveling more, having more fun.

Gratitude directly counteracts this. When you practice noticing and appreciating what you have, you're training your brain away from the comparison trap. You're shifting from "I don't have what they have" to "Look at what I do have."

This isn't about settling for less or not wanting to improve. It's about recognizing that constant comparison makes you perpetually dissatisfied no matter how much you achieve or acquire. There's always someone with more. The goalpost always moves.

Gratitude anchors you in your actual experience rather than someone else's curated presentation. It's not "I should be happy with less than I deserve." It's "I can appreciate what I have while working toward what I want."

Gratitude in Difficult Times

Here's where gratitude gets real: how do you practice it when things are genuinely terrible?

You don't pretend everything is fine. You don't force fake positivity. You don't dismiss your pain.

Instead, you look for what remains good even when much is wrong. This might be:

- People who show up for you
- Your own strength in facing difficulty
- Small comforts (hot shower, good meal, comfortable bed)
- Moments of relief or reprieve
- Your capacity to feel, even when feelings hurt
- Whatever beauty or kindness still exists alongside the hardship

This is Viktor Frankl's approach in the concentration camps: finding meaning and moments of grace even in hell. Not because hell isn't hell, but because noticing what remains good is how you survive hell.

One of my lowest periods, I kept a gratitude practice that was mostly "I'm grateful I got through today. I'm grateful I have a bed to sleep in. I'm grateful I can still feel things even though it hurts." Tiny, basic things. But that practice was a lifeline. It's a daily reminder that not everything was destroyed, that something still worked, that I could still notice goodness even when surrounded by difficulty.

That's not toxic positivity. That's survival.

The 21-Day Gratitude Protocol

Building gratitude as a habit requires consistency and structure. Here's your 21-day challenge:

Days 1-7: Basic Practice

- Each evening, write down three specific things you're grateful for from that day
- Make them specific, not generic
- Notice the feelings that arise, don't force fake enthusiasm

- When struggling, include basics: "I have food and shelter. My body's functioning."

Days 8-14: Expansion

- Continue the basic practice
- Add one gratitude letter (written but not sent)
- Try one gratitude walk
- Practice savoring at least one positive moment each day

Days 15-21: Integration

- Continue basic practice
- Try obstacle gratitude: what's one thing you're learning from current challenges?
- Share gratitude with one person directly (not performatively, genuinely)
- Are you noticing positive things more automatically?

Troubleshooting:

- If it feels fake, you're probably being too generic. Get more specific.
- If you can't find anything, you're looking for big things. Look smaller.
- If you're resisting, acknowledge the resistance and do it anyway. Resistance is just your brain protecting its current patterns.
- If it's not changing anything after a week, you're probably performing it rather than genuinely practicing it. Go deeper.

Gratitude as Resource Management

Here's the strategic argument for gratitude that has nothing to do with spirituality or positivity:

You have finite emotional resources. You need those resources to face difficulties, solve problems, and maintain relationships. When you're emotionally depleted, which happens when you focus exclusively on what's wrong, you have nothing left for effective action.

Gratitude is resource management. It's actively maintaining the emotional reserves you need to stay engaged. Not by denying problems, but by ensuring that problems aren't the only things you're attending to.

Think of it like financial management. If you only track expenses without ever acknowledging income, you'll feel perpetually broke even if your net worth is positive. Gratitude is acknowledging the income. You don't ignore expenses, but to you get an accurate picture of your actual resources.

You can't fix problems from a place of total depletion. You need enough emotional fuel to keep going. Gratitude generates that fuel.

The Revolution

Here's why this is revolutionary and not just self-help fluff:

We live in a culture engineered to keep you dissatisfied. Capitalism profits from your sense of lack. Media profits from your outrage. Social media profits from your envy. The entire system runs on keeping you focused on what's missing, what's wrong, what you don't have.

Gratitude is rebellion against that system. It's reclaiming your attention from forces that want to monetize your dissatisfaction. It's saying "I see what's wrong AND I see what's good" instead of letting others control your perception.

This doesn't mean accepting injustice. It means maintaining the emotional and psychological resources to fight injustice without being consumed by despair.

Grateful people aren't complacent. They're sustained. They can stay in the fight because they're not running on empty. They can see problems clearly because they haven't lost sight of what's worth protecting.

That's the revolution. Not fake positivity. Not ignoring reality. But refusing to let your perception be colonized by forces that profit from your misery.

Practice gratitude. Not because everything is fine, but because you need the strength to face what isn't.

9

Connection as Antidote

I have 847 friends on Facebook, follow 312 people on Instagram, and have ongoing text conversations with maybe a dozen people at any given time. I am, by modern metrics, extremely connected.

I am also, on many days, profoundly lonely.

Not the dramatic loneliness of being stranded on a desert island. The subtle, chronic loneliness of being surrounded by people but not truly seen by any of them. Of having hundreds of digital connections but no one to call at 3 AM. Of sharing curated highlights with an audience but not sharing actual struggles with actual humans.

This is the paradox of our age: we have more tools for connection than any generation in history, and we're experiencing an epidemic of loneliness that's literally killing people.

The research is clear and brutal: strong social connections are among the most significant predictors of happiness, health, and longevity. Meanwhile, chronic loneliness increases mortality risk as much as smoking fifteen cigarettes a day. It's not poetic exaggeration. It's epidemiology.

We're dying from disconnection while scrolling through endless feeds of other people's connection performances.

Something has gone catastrophically wrong, and we need to talk about how to fix it.

The Loneliness Epidemic

Here's what the data shows: rates of loneliness have been climbing for decades. More people live alone. Fewer people report having close friends. Community participation has plummeted. The number of Americans who say they have no one to discuss important matters with has tripled since 1985.

This isn't about being introverted or preferring solitude. Those are fine. This is about involuntary isolation and the absence of meaningful connection when you actually want it.

The health consequences are staggering. Loneliness increases risk of cardiovascular disease, dementia, stroke, depression, and anxiety. It weakens immune function and increases inflammation. Lonely people sleep worse, heal slower, and die younger.

And before you think this is just about elderly people in nursing homes, young adults report the highest rates of loneliness. The generation that grew up most connected digitally feels most disconnected personally.

The tools that promised to bring us together have, in many ways, driven us further apart.

Why Digital Connection Isn't Enough

I'm not going to tell you social media is evil or that online connection is worthless. I've had meaningful exchanges online. I've maintained long-distance friendships through technology. I've found communities around niche interests that don't exist in my physical location.

But here's the thing: digital connection doesn't fully substitute for in-person presence. And pretending it does is making us sick.

When you're with someone physically, your nervous systems synchronize. You unconsciously mirror each other's breathing, movements, and expressions. You pick up on micro-expressions, tone shifts, and energy that video calls can't capture. You share space and time in a way that creates a different kind of intimacy.

There's something about looking into another person's actual eyes and not their pixelated representation on a screen. This interaction meets a need that texting simply doesn't. There's something about being in the same room, breathing the same air, existing in the same physical moment that creates bonds digital interaction can't replicate.

Think about it. When you're struggling, what do you actually want? A supportive text, or someone sitting with you in silence? A heart emoji on your post, or someone bringing you dinner? A video call, or a hug?

Digital tools are valuable for maintaining connection across distance and for initial contact. But they're supplements to in-person connection, not replacements for it. When they become substitutes, we end up malnourished.

The Vulnerability Problem

Here's an uncomfortable truth: real connection requires vulnerability, and vulnerability is terrifying.

Our culture worships independence and self-sufficiency. Needing people is weakness. Having your shit together means handling everything alone. We curate perfect public personas while hiding our actual struggles, fears, and needs.

The result? We're surrounded by people also hiding behind perfect facades, everyone feeling alone in their imperfection, no one willing to be the first to admit they're struggling.

Real friendship requires showing up as you actually are. Messy sure, uncertain, sometimes struggling, sometimes needing help. It requires asking for support and admitting you don't have it all figured out. It requires being seen, really seen, in your actual humanity rather than your curated highlight reel.

This is scary as hell. What if they judge you? What if they reject you? What if your real self isn't enough?

But here's what's scarier: a lifetime of surface-level connections that never go deep enough to actually sustain you. A lifetime of pretending you're fine while slowly suffocating from loneliness. A lifetime of protection from vulnerability that's also protection from genuine intimacy.

You can have safety or you can have connection. You can't have both in their absolute forms. Real connection requires accepting some risk.

Deepening Existing Relationships

Most of us don't need more friends. We need deeper friendships. Here's how to go deeper with people already in your life:

Create rituals of connection. Regular, predictable times you connect: weekly dinners, monthly hikes, standing coffee dates. Rituals build consistency and signal that the relationship matters enough to prioritize.

Ask better questions. Move past "How are you?" (reflexive "fine") to specific questions: "What's been hard this week?" "What are you excited about?" "What's on your mind lately?" Questions that invite actual sharing.

Be present without fixing. When someone shares a struggle, resist the urge to immediately offer solutions. Just listen. Just be with them in it. Sometimes presence is the help.

Share your own struggles. Don't just perform success. Let people see you uncertain, struggling, needing support. This gives them permission to do the same and creates space for real intimacy.

Offer and receive support concretely. Not "let me know if you need anything" (they won't) but "I'm bringing dinner Tuesday, what do you want?" Be specific in offering. And when offered help, practice saying yes.

Celebrate together. Share good things, not just struggles. Joy shared multiplies. Make time for celebration, play, and shared delight.

Making New Friends as Adults

Making friends as a kid was easy: proximity plus time equals friendship. You sat next to someone in class repeatedly and boom, friends.

As adults, it's weirdly harder. Here's how to do it anyway:

Show up repeatedly to the same places. Join something. Anything. A class, a volunteer organization, a sports team, a book club, a community garden. The key is consistency. Friendship requires repeated casual contact over time. You can't force instant intimacy, but you can create conditions where it develops naturally.

Be the initiator. Someone has to suggest coffee, exchange numbers, propose plans. Be that person. Yes, you risk rejection. Do it anyway. Most people want more connection but are waiting for someone else to make the first move.

Start from shared interests or values. It's easier to connect with people doing something you both care about than to manufacture connection from nothing. Find your people by going where your people are.

Accept different depths. Not every friendship needs to be soul-baring intimacy. Casual friendships. People you see at the gym, chat with at the coffee shop, connect with around a specific shared activity also matter. They provide a sense of belonging and community even if they're not your emergency contact.

Give it time. Friendship researchers estimate it takes roughly 200 hours of time together to develop a close friendship. You're not going to have a best friend after two coffee dates. Be patient. Keep showing up.

Different Types of Connection

You need variety in your relationship ecosystem:

Intimate friendships: Deep, reciprocal relationships where you're fully seen and supported. These are your emergency contacts, your vulnerability-safe people. You probably only need a few of these.

Casual friendships: People you enjoy but don't share everything with. The friend you play tennis with, the person you chat with at volunteer events. These provide lighter connection and sense of community.

Community belonging: Being part of something larger, a neighborhood, a faith community, a movement, an organization. This provides identity and purpose beyond individual relationships.

Purposeful collaboration: Working together toward shared goals. This creates connection through joint effort and shared meaning.

You need some combination of all of these. If you only have one type, you're missing something.

Digital Connection Done Right

Technology isn't the enemy. Misuse of technology is the enemy. Here's how to use it wisely:

Use digital tools to enhance in-person relationships, not replace them. Text to coordinate meeting up. Video call when you can't be together physically. Share things that will make them laugh. But don't let digital communication become a substitute for actual presence.

Recognize when online communities genuinely serve you. Sometimes online connection is the only available option—geographic isolation, rare conditions, niche interests, marginalized identities finding community. These can be genuinely sustaining. But notice whether they're enhancing your life or substituting for what you're missing.

Notice the quality of your digital interactions. Active engagement (actual conversations, meaningful exchanges) enhances wellbeing. Passive consumption (lurking, scrolling, comparing) tends to increase loneliness and depression. Adjust accordingly.

Set boundaries around digital pseudo-connection. If you're using social media scrolling as a substitute for calling a friend, stop scrolling and call the friend. If you're numbing loneliness with infinite feeds, close the app and address the loneliness directly.

10

Purpose Beyond Performance

I spent my twenties chasing achievement, convinced that purpose came from accomplishment. Get the degree, land the job, publish the articles, build the career, achieve the goals. Each milestone was supposed to deliver that sense of meaning I was searching for.

Spoiler alert. It didn't.

I'd hit a goal, feel briefly satisfied, then immediately pivot to the next target. The goalposts kept moving. The accomplishments accumulated but the sense of "this matters" remained elusive. I was productive as hell and completely hollow.

At some point, lying awake at 2 AM after a professionally successful day that felt emotionally empty, I realized I'd been asking the wrong question. The question wasn't "What should I achieve?" It was "What do I actually care about?"

Those are radically different questions that lead to radically different lives.

Purpose Is Not Productivity

Our culture has conflated purpose with productivity so thoroughly that most people can't distinguish between them.

We measure worth by output. Value by accomplishment. Meaning by what you've achieved, produced, or accumulated. If you're not constantly doing, building, achieving, or advancing, you're wasting your life. Your purpose, we're told, should be your career. Your meaning should come from your success.

This is bullshit, and it's making us miserable.

Productivity is about output, how much you produce, how efficiently you produce it, how much value (usually economic) that production generates.

Purpose is about meaning. It's what you care about, what you're oriented toward, what gives your actions significance beyond their immediate results.

You can be incredibly productive while living a purposeless life. You can produce endless output that means nothing to you, achieve goals that don't actually matter to you, succeed by every external metric while feeling internally empty.

And you can have deep purpose while not being particularly productive in conventional terms. Raising children, caring for aging parents, maintaining friendships, engaging with community, creating art no one sees, pursuing understanding for its own sake, these things create profound meaning without necessarily producing marketable output.

The question isn't "What can I achieve?" It's "What do I care about deeply enough to orient my life around it?"

What Actually Creates Meaning

Research from positive psychology and existential philosophy converges on several sources of meaning:

Connection to something larger than yourself. Being part of something that extends beyond your individual existence like a community, a tradition, a movement, a lineage, nature, humanity. This contextualizes your life within a bigger story.

Contributing to others. Making someone else's life better, easier, or more bearable. This can be grand (inventing something) or small (being there for a friend). The scale matters less than the reality of positive impact.

Living your values. Actually aligning your daily choices with what you believe matters. This isn't about perfect consistency. It's about the felt sense that your actions reflect what you care about.

Creating or understanding. Making something, art, ideas, solutions, beauty. Or pursuing understanding for its own sake. The drive to create and comprehend appears to be fundamentally human and fundamentally meaningful.

Confronting challenge with courage. You find purpose not just in pleasure or achievement but in how you respond to struggle.

Notice what's missing from this list: achievement, success, wealth, status, productivity. Those might be side effects of purposeful living, but they're not the source of meaning.

Your Values, Not Their Expectations

Here's an exercise: Write down what you actually value. Not what you think you should value. Not what your parents, culture, or Instagram feed says you should value. What you actually care about when you're honest with yourself.

Maybe it's: **Connection. Creativity. Learning. Justice. Beauty. Adventure. Stability. Contribution. Freedom. Growth. Pleasure. Integrity. Play.**

Your list will be unique. There's no universal set of correct values. The question is: are you living according to yours?

Most people have never done this inventory. They're living according to values they absorbed from family, culture, or circumstance without ever examining whether those values actually resonate. They're pursuing someone else's definition of purpose and wondering why it feels empty.

Purpose isn't found in some grand revelation. It's found in the unglamorous work of figuring out what you actually care about and then making choices that align with it.

This might mean: taking a lower-paying job that aligns with your values, prioritizing relationships over career advancement, choosing creativity over stability, valuing rest over constant productivity, pursuing understanding over prestige.

It definitely means tolerating the discomfort of other people thinking you're making the wrong choices. Because purpose is personal, and what's meaningful to you won't make sense to everyone else.

Multiple Scales of Purpose

Purpose anxiety often comes from thinking you need one singular capital-P Purpose—your life's calling, your grand contribution, your reason for existing.

This is too much pressure and also not how meaning actually works.

Purpose exists at multiple scales simultaneously:

Micro-purpose: The meaning in this specific moment. Listening fully to someone who's struggling. Making dinner with care. Noticing beauty on your walk. Being kind to the checkout person. These moments of aligned presence create meaning regardless of bigger context.

Relational purpose: The meaning in your relationships and roles. Being a good friend, parent, partner, neighbor, colleague. Showing up for people. Building and maintaining connections. These create ongoing purpose through how you exist in relation to others.

Community purpose: Meaning through participation in something collective. Contributing to your neighborhood, working toward shared goals, being part of movements or organizations. Purpose through belonging and collective effort.

Legacy purpose: Longer-term projects and commitments. Building something, fighting for something, creating something that outlasts you. This is the "big P" Purpose people often fixate on, but it's just one scale, not the only scale.

You don't need to have legacy purpose figured out to have a meaningful life. If you're living with micro-purpose (present, aligned, engaged) and relational purpose (showing up for people), you're already living meaningfully.

The big projects might emerge from that foundation, or they might not. Either way, your life has purpose.

Engagement as Meaning

Mihaly Csikszentmihalyi's research on "flow" reveals something crucial: engagement itself creates meaning.

Flow is that state of absorption in challenging activity where you lose track of time, your skills are stretched but not overwhelmed, you're fully present and focused. It feels intrinsically rewarding regardless of outcome.

This suggests meaning isn't just about grand purposes or final results but the quality of your engagement with whatever you're doing.

You can find meaning in: solving a difficult problem, making music, having a deep conversation, building something with your hands, understanding a complex idea, playing a sport, creating art, teaching someone a skill.

The activity matters less than the quality of absorption in it. When you're fully engaged, challenged but capable, present and focused, you're experiencing meaning in real-time.

This is why people can find profound purpose in activities that don't look "important" by conventional measures. The woodworker absorbed in their craft, the cook lost in creating a meal, the gardener tending plants, they're experiencing meaning through engagement, regardless of whether their activity produces achievement or recognition.

Purpose isn't just about what you do but how you do it.

Purpose in the Face of Mortality

Here's the existential crisis at the heart of purpose questions: we're all going to die. Everything we build will eventually crumble. The universe doesn't care about our achievements. In the face of eventual oblivion, what's the point of anything?

Two possible responses:

Nihilism: Nothing ultimately matters, so nothing matters at all. This leads to paralysis and despair.

Existentialism: Nothing has inherent ultimate meaning, so we're free to create meaning. Impermanence doesn't negate significance but intensifies it.

I lean toward the second one, obviously, but let me make the case:

The fact that your life is finite doesn't make it meaningless. It makes it precious. S precious. You have limited time, which means how you spend that time actually matters. If you lived forever, you could defer everything indefinitely. Mortality creates urgency and significance.

The fact that everything eventually ends doesn't erase the reality of your experience now. The meal you shared with friends wasn't meaningless just because it ended. The relationship that sustained you for years isn't meaningless just because it eventually changed. The meaning was in the experience itself, not in its permanence.

And the fact that the universe doesn't inherently care about your choices means you're free to decide what matters to you. You're not trying to fulfill some cosmic plan but you're authoring your own meaning.

This is terrifying (no ultimate blueprint to follow) and liberating (you get to decide what counts as a life well-lived).

Living Purposefully Without Having It All Figured Out

You don't need to have your entire life purpose mapped out to live meaningfully today. Here's how to proceed without certainty:

Start with what you know. What do you care about right now? What feels meaningful in this chapter of your life? Start there. Purpose evolves. What matters at 25 might not matter at 45. That's fine.

Follow resonance. Pay attention to what energizes you versus what depletes you. What conversations leave you feeling more alive? What activities create that sense of "yes, this"? Move toward those things.

Align daily choices with current values. You don't need to know your ultimate purpose to make today's choices reflect what matters to you now. This is purposeful living even without perfect clarity about the future.

Embrace exploration. Not knowing your purpose yet isn't failure but an invitation to explore. Try things. See what resonates. Purpose often emerges through engagement, not before it.

Accept evolution. Your purpose will change as you change. It's growth. The purpose that sustained you through one chapter might not fit the next. Let it evolve.

Finding Meaning in Ordinary Life

The pressure to have an extraordinary purpose makes ordinary life feel insufficient. But here's the truth: most meaning happens in ordinary moments.

The conversation with your kid at breakfast. The friend you texted to check on. The work you did with care even though no one's watching. The small beauty you noticed on your commute. The kindness you offered a stranger. The value you lived even when it was inconvenient.

These aren't failures to achieve grand purpose but are purpose enacted at the scale of daily life.

Meaning doesn't require extraordinary circumstances or achievements. It requires presence, alignment, and engagement with what's actually in front of you.

Your ordinary life, all the relationships, the small choices, the daily practices, the moments of connection and beauty and struggle, is where purpose actually lives. Not in some future achievement or grand accomplishment, but here, now, in how you show up for what's real.

Reconnecting When You Feel Lost

Sometimes you lose the thread. The things that felt meaningful stop resonating. You feel disconnected from purpose, adrift.

This is normal. It's not permanent. Here's how to find your way back:

Return to your body. Purpose often lives in physical experience of what makes you feel energized, alive, engaged. Get out of your head and into sensation.

Reconnect with people. Meaning often emerges through relationship. Reach out. Have real conversations. Be present with someone you care about.

Do small meaningful things. Don't wait for big purpose to return. Do something small that aligns with your values today. Alignment in small choices can reignite larger purpose.

Examine what you're avoiding. Sometimes losing purpose is about avoiding something difficult. What conversation needs having? What truth needs facing? What change needs making?

Give it time. Periods of uncertainty and disconnection are part of the process. You're not broken. You're in transition. Keep showing up. Purpose often returns when you stop forcing it.

The Point

You don't need to solve world hunger or cure cancer to have a purposeful life. You don't need to achieve greatness or leave a massive legacy. You don't need to have it all figured out.

You need to know what you care about and let that guide your choices. You need to show up for relationships with presence. You need to engage with what's in front of you. You need to live your values at the scale of daily life.

That's purpose. Not in some distant future achievement, but here, now, in how you exist in the world.

Your life has meaning not because of what you accomplish but because of what you care about and how you live accordingly.

That's enough. You're enough.
Now stop reading and go do something that matters to you.

11

Taking Meaningful Action

Here's what doomscrolling never tells you! Reading about problems is not the same as addressing problems. Feeling bad about injustice is not the same as fighting injustice. Being aware of suffering is not the same as alleviating suffering.

I spent years confusing consumption with contribution. I'd scroll through crisis after crisis, feel appropriately terrible about each one, share a few posts to signal that I cared, and then? Do absolutely nothing. I was "staying informed" and "raising awareness" while remaining completely inactive in any material sense.

I felt like I was engaged with the world's problems. I was actually just marinating in them.

The shift happened when I realized that all this consuming wasn't helping anyone, not the people suffering from the problems I was reading about, and certainly not me. If anything, it was making me less capable of helping because I was depleted, paralyzed, and convinced that nothing I could do would matter anyway.

Turns out, taking even small action is infinitely more effective at combating despair than consuming infinite information about why you should despair.

Action as Antidote to Helplessness

Research on learned helplessness shows something crucial: the antidote isn't positive thinking or reframing or even understanding. The antidote is action that produces results.

When you take action and see it create change, even small change, you build evidence that you're not powerless. Your brain learns: "I did something. Something happened. My actions matter."

This is why doom-scrolling is so psychologically destructive. You're exposing yourself to hundreds of problems you can't solve, training your brain in helplessness with each scroll. "Here's a problem. I can't do anything about it. Here's another problem. I can't do anything about that either. Here's another…"

Your nervous system concludes: "I am helpless in the face of overwhelming catastrophe." And then you wonder why you feel hopeless.

Action breaks this cycle. Even small action. Or imperfect action. Because action, any action that creates any result, reminds your brain that you have agency.

You can't solve global poverty. But you can volunteer at a food bank and see people eat because you showed up. You can't fix the climate crisis alone. But you can organize a neighborhood tree-planting and see new trees because you acted. You can't end all suffering. But you can check on your lonely neighbor and see their face light up because you cared.

These aren't failures to solve everything. They're evidence that action matters.

Practical Optimism: Hope as Fuel

There are two kinds of optimism. One is passive: "Everything will work out somehow." This leads to complacency.

The other is active—what I call practical optimism: "Positive outcomes are possible if I engage." This leads to action.

Practical optimism doesn't require certainty. You don't need to know you'll succeed to take action. You just need to believe that:

1. Your effort might make a difference
2. Trying is better than not trying
3. Staying engaged keeps possibilities open that despair closes

This is hope as fuel rather than hope as fantasy. You're not waiting for things to magically improve. You're acting because action is how things improve, even when improvement isn't guaranteed.

The pessimist says: "Things probably won't work out, so why try?" The practical optimist says: "Things might not work out, which is exactly why I need to try."

Same uncertainty, opposite response, completely different outcome.

Finding Your Meaningful Action

Not all action is meaningful. Some action is performative. Sure, you do it to look good, to alleviate guilt, to signal virtue. It might create some good, but it's not sustaining because it's not genuinely yours.

Meaningful action comes from genuine care. Here's how to find yours:

Start with your actual concerns. Not what you think you should care about. Not what everyone else is focused on. What genuinely keeps you up at night? What injustice actually makes you angry? What suffering do you genuinely feel moved to address?

Look at your sphere of influence. Where do you actually have capacity to create change? Your family? Your workplace? Your neighborhood? Your specific skills or resources? Start where you have leverage, not where you just have concern.

Consider your natural tendencies. Are you a one-on-one person or a systems person? Do you prefer direct service or advocacy? Are you energized by people or by solo work? Your action should match your wiring, not fight against it.

Ask what needs doing that you're positioned to do. Not what needs doing in general (everything), but what needs doing that your specific combination of skills, resources, location, and interests positions you to address.

The intersection of what you genuinely care about, where you have influence, what matches your temperament, and what you're positioned to do is where you'll find sustainable, meaningful action.

Modes of Action: Many Ways to Contribute

Action doesn't mean one thing. There are multiple valid approaches:

Direct service: Helping individuals directly. Volunteering at a shelter, tutoring kids, visiting isolated elders, delivering meals. You see immediate impact. You help specific people. This is deeply satisfying for people who need to see tangible results.

Systemic change: Working on root causes. Organizing, advocacy, policy change, changing systems that create problems in the first place. This is slower, harder to see results, but potentially addresses problems at scale. For people who think structurally.

Cultural shift: Changing narratives, norms, and consciousness. Creating art, writing, having conversations, modeling different ways of being. This is subtle and long-term but shapes what becomes possible. For people who work through meaning and story.

Personal integrity: Living according to your values in daily choices. How you spend money, what you consume, how you treat people, what you normalize through your behavior. This is quiet but cumulative. For people who believe individual choices matter.

You don't have to choose one. You can engage through multiple modes. But knowing these exist helps you recognize that if traditional activism doesn't fit you, there are other ways to contribute.

Overcoming Action Paralysis

The biggest obstacle to action isn't apathy but paralysis. You care, but you're frozen by:

Everything-or-nothing thinking: "If I can't solve the whole problem, there's no point in doing anything." This is perfectionism disguised as morality. It keeps you pure and uninvolved rather than imperfect and engaged.

Too many options: When everything seems urgent, nothing feels manageable. You're paralyzed by choice, unable to prioritize because prioritizing means not choosing something else.

Fear of inadequacy: Whatever you do won't be enough. You could always do more. Someone else is doing more. Your contribution is a drop in the ocean.

Uncertainty about outcomes: What if your action doesn't work? What if you make things worse? What if you waste your effort?

Here's how to break through:

Start ridiculously small. Don't try to solve anything. Just do one tiny thing. Make one phone call. Attend one meeting. Donate $10. Send one letter. Tiny action breaks paralysis and builds momentum.

Choose one thing. Not everything. One thing. You can't address all problems. You can address one. Pick the one that calls to you most strongly and focus there. You can always add more later.

Accept imperfection. Your action will be imperfect. You'll make mistakes. You'll learn as you go. Do it anyway. Imperfect action beats perfect inaction every single time.

Focus on process, not outcome. You can't control results. You can control effort. Measure yourself by "did I show up and try?" not "did I solve everything?"

Remember: you're not the only one acting. You're not responsible for solving everything alone. You're responsible for your part. When many people do their parts, change happens. Your drop combines with other drops to become the ocean.

Matching Action to Your Reality

103

Your action should fit your actual life, not some idealized version of engagement:

If you're introverted: Focus on behind-the-scenes work, written advocacy, one-on-one support, research, creating resources. You don't have to attend protests or work a crowd to contribute meaningfully.

If you're extroverted: Channel that energy into organizing, outreach, building coalitions, facilitating groups, mobilizing people. You're wired for collective action.

If you have limited time: Micro-actions matter. Monthly donations, voting, signing petitions, making ethical purchasing choices, having one conversation. Don't let limited time become an excuse for zero action.

If you have limited money: Time, skills, voice, and presence are also valuable. Show up. Share knowledge. Amplify others. Connect people. Build community.

If you have caregiving responsibilities: Include kids in age-appropriate action. Find ways to combine caregiving with contribution. Connect with other caregivers. Your constraints are real! Work within them, not despite them.

If you have chronic illness or disability: Pace yourself. Contribute when and how you can. Rest is also resistance against systems that demand constant productivity. Your worth isn't measured by your capacity for action.

Sustainability: The Long Game

Burnout doesn't help anyone. Here's how to pace yourself for sustained engagement:

Build sustainable practices, not heroic efforts. Better to do a little consistently than a lot in unsustainable bursts followed by collapse. Marathon, not sprint.

Protect your resources. You can't pour from an empty cup. Rest, recharge, maintain your own wellbeing. This is strategic, not selfish.

Celebrate small wins. Don't wait for total victory to acknowledge progress. Notice and appreciate incremental change. This sustains motivation.

Connect with others. Shared action is more sustainable than solo action. You carry each other through hard stretches. You celebrate together. You're less likely to burn out in community.

Give yourself permission to step back. Sometimes you need to reduce engagement to recover capacity. This is pacing. You can't stay in high gear indefinitely.

Remember your why. When you're exhausted, reconnect with why this matters to you. Not obligation, not guilt, but genuine care. That's what sustains long-term action.

Handling Inadequacy and Guilt

You will feel like you're not doing enough. Here's the truth: you're never doing enough by some absolute standard because there's no limit to what needs doing.

The question isn't "Am I doing enough?" It's "Am I doing what I can, given my actual circumstances and capacities, in a sustainable way that allows me to keep showing up?"

If yes, that's enough.

You're not responsible for solving everything. You're responsible for your honest contribution. That looks different for everyone based on resources, constraints, and circumstances.

Someone with more resources might contribute more. Someone with fewer constraints might engage more intensively. That's not a judgment on your worth. It's just reality.

Do what you can, with what you have, where you are. That's the standard. Not perfection. Not martyrdom. Just honest engagement.

Your Action Plan

Here's your framework:

Identify one area of genuine concern. What actually matters to you? Just one thing.

Assess your sphere of influence. Do you have actual capacity to impact?

Choose one action. What's one concrete thing you could do this week?

Take that action. Do it imperfectly. Do it scared without knowing if it'll work. Just do it.

Assess and adjust. What happened? What did you learn? What's the next small step?

Repeat. Build from there. Add more as capacity allows. But start with one thing.

The Alternative

The alternative to action is continuing to doomscroll, feeling helpless, and being consumed by problems you're not addressing.

That's not "staying informed." That's choosing despair.

Action, even small, imperfect, uncertain action, is choosing engagement over paralysis. It's choosing agency over helplessness. It's choosing to be part of solutions rather than just aware of problems.

Your action might not solve everything. It will definitely help someone or something. And it will absolutely help you by reminding you that you're not powerless, that your choices matter, that engagement is possible.

Stop scrolling.

Start doing.

Imperfect action beats perfect inaction.

Every. Single. Time.

Rewriting Your Narrative

For years, my dominant narrative was: "I'm fundamentally broken and everything I touch eventually falls apart."

This story had evidence. Failed relationships? See, I'm broken. Career setbacks? Told you. Everything I touch falls apart. Friendships that faded? More proof. My brain collected data points that confirmed the narrative while conveniently ignoring everything that contradicted it.

The story felt true. It felt like insight, like I was finally seeing myself clearly. It felt like the honest, unflinching assessment of reality that everyone else was too optimistic or deluded to acknowledge.

It was also completely fucking me over.

Because here's what stories do: they don't just describe reality. They create it. When you believe you're broken, you act like someone who's broken. When you believe everything you touch falls apart, you either stop touching things or you unconsciously sabotage them to confirm your narrative. When you believe you're powerless, you don't exercise what power you actually have.

The story becomes self-fulfilling. And then you point to the results as proof that the story was true all along.

This chapter is about recognizing that the stories you tell yourself are just that. Stories. Interpretations, not facts. And interpretations can be revised.

How Narratives Work

Your brain is a meaning-making machine. It takes the raw data of experience and weaves it into narratives, which are stories that explain who you are, how the world works, and what things mean.

But here's the crucial part! These narratives are selective and interpretive.

Selective means your brain chooses which details to include and which to ignore. Out of everything that happens to you, you notice and remember the parts that fit your existing story while filtering out parts that don't.

Interpretive means your brain assigns meaning to events, and those meanings aren't inherent in the events themselves. You don't experience objective reality. You experience your interpretation of reality.

Think about a job rejection. The facts: you applied, they said no. But the story your brain tells about those facts? That's interpretation. "I'm not good enough" is a story. "They chose someone with different qualifications" is a different story. "This wasn't the right fit" is another. Same facts, completely different narratives, radically different emotional and behavioral consequences.

And here's what makes this powerful: narratives aren't static. You're constantly revising them, usually unconsciously, as new experiences either confirm or challenge your existing stories.

Which means they can be revised consciously and intentionally too.

Identifying Your Doom Loop Stories

Most of us are running narratives we've never examined. They're just the water we swim in, the lens we see through, the "truth" we never question.

Here are some common doom loop narratives. See if any sound familiar:

"I'm powerless." Nothing I do makes a real difference. The forces shaping my life are beyond my control. I'm just a victim of circumstances.

"Nothing I do matters." Even when I try, it doesn't change anything. My efforts are futile. I'm insignificant in the grand scheme.

"The world is going to hell." Everything is getting worse. Humanity is doomed. There's no hope for positive change.

"People are fundamentally selfish." Everyone's out for themselves. Trust is naive. Kindness is weakness or performance.

"I'm broken/damaged/unworthy." Something is fundamentally wrong with me. I'm not enough. I'm too much. I'm irreparably flawed.

"Good things don't last." Any positive development is temporary. Waiting for the other shoe to drop. Happiness is fleeting, suffering is permanent.

"I always fuck things up." I'm the common denominator in my failures. I self-sabotage. Success isn't available to me.

These are interpretations masquerading as facts. And they're incredibly powerful because they shape everything: what you notice, how you interpret it, what you expect, and how you behave.

Where Stories Come From

Your narratives aren't random. They come from somewhere:

Personal experience: Especially early experiences and trauma. If you grew up in chaos, you might develop a narrative that the world is unpredictable and dangerous. If you experienced betrayal, you might develop a story that people can't be trusted.

Family messages: The explicit and implicit stories your family told about who you are and how the world works. "You're so sensitive." "Life is hard." "People like us don't succeed." "Don't get your hopes up."

Cultural conditioning: The narratives your culture, media, and society reinforce. Narratives about success, worth, gender, race, class, what's possible and what isn't.

Trauma: Traumatic experiences often create rigid narratives as a protection mechanism. Your brain creates a story that explains what happened and how to prevent it from happening again, even when that story is inaccurate or limiting.

Media consumption: The stories you're exposed to constantly shape your own narratives. If your media diet is all doom and crisis, that becomes your narrative about reality.

Understanding where your narratives come from doesn't excuse them, but it does help you see they're not inevitable truths about you or the world—they're learned interpretations that can be unlearned.

Techniques for Narrative Revision

Find counterexamples. Your dominant narrative says "I always fuck things up." Okay. Find times when you didn't. They exist but you've just been filtering them out. This isn't about denying failures;

it's about getting a complete picture instead of a selectively negative one.

Identify alternative interpretations. For any event, there are multiple possible meanings. You got rejected? Could be you're not good enough (your current story). Could also be bad timing, wrong fit, they had an internal candidate, your approach didn't match their needs, you need different skills you can develop. Which interpretation is most accurate and most empowering?

Question the evidence. You believe people are fundamentally selfish. What's the evidence? Be specific. Now, what's the evidence against? Friends who showed up for you. Strangers who helped. People who volunteer, donate, care for others. Are you seeing the full picture or just the parts that confirm your narrative?

Test the narrative. What if your story is wrong? What would change if you operated from a different story for a week? Try it. Treat it as an experiment. See what happens.

Author new stories. Write a different version of your story that's still true to the facts but interprets them differently. Not fantasy but truth from a different angle.

Rewriting vs. Denying Reality

Here's the critical distinction: rewriting your narrative isn't about denial or toxic positivity.

Denial says: "Nothing bad happened. I'm fine. Everything is fine."

Narrative revision says: "Something difficult happened. Here's a more complete and empowering way to understand it."

You're not erasing struggles or pretending problems don't exist. You're refusing to let one interpretation of those struggles define everything.

Example: You went through a difficult breakup.

Doom narrative: "I'm unlovable. Relationships always fail. I'm going to be alone forever."

Revised narrative: "This relationship ended. It was painful. I'm learning what I need in partnerships. I'm capable of connection, as evidenced by the fact that I connected deeply enough to be hurt by the loss. I'm resilient enough to survive this and open to connection again when I'm ready."

Both versions acknowledge the breakup. One interpretation destroys you. The other leaves you intact and open to future possibility.

That's the difference.

Common Cognitive Distortions

Your narratives are often built on thinking errors, essentially cognitive distortions that feel logical but are actually just bad reasoning:

All-or-nothing thinking: Everything is black and white, success or failure, perfect or worthless. "If I'm not amazing at this, I'm terrible at it."

Overgeneralization: One negative event becomes a universal pattern. "This happened once, therefore it always happens."

Mental filtering: You focus exclusively on negatives while ignoring positives. Out of ten interactions, one was negative and that's the only one you remember and replay.

Catastrophizing: Assuming the worst possible outcome. "I made a mistake, therefore I'll get fired, lose my house, and die alone."

Personalization: Taking responsibility for things outside your control. "Someone was rude to me; it must be because I did something wrong" (maybe they're just having a bad day).

Learn to catch these in real-time. When you notice yourself spiraling into a doom narrative, ask: "What thinking error am I making right now?"

Usually it's one of these. Usually reality is more nuanced than your catastrophic interpretation.

Identity Narratives: Who You Think You Are

The deepest and most powerful narratives are about identity, who you believe you fundamentally are.

"I'm a victim." "I'm a survivor." "I'm broken." "I'm resilient." "I'm unlucky." "I'm capable." "I'm unworthy." "I'm enough."

These identity stories shape everything because they determine what feels possible for you. If you believe you're fundamentally broken, you can't imagine being whole. If you believe you're inherently unlucky, you can't sustain optimism. If you believe you're unworthy, you'll sabotage opportunities.

Identity narratives often feel like truth because they're so embedded. "This is just who I am." But they're still just stories, just interpretations of your experiences, not fixed realities.

You're not "just" anything. You're complex, changing, capable of growth and revision. The version of yourself you've been performing isn't the only version available.

The Self-Fulfilling Prophecy Problem

Here's why narrative revision matters so much. Your stories don't just describe your reality. They create it.

If you believe you're powerless, you don't try to change things. Your lack of effort produces lack of results. The lack of results confirms your belief in powerlessness. The cycle reinforces itself.

If you believe nothing you do matters, you either don't do things or you do them half-heartedly. Predictably, they don't matter much. Your belief is confirmed.

If you believe you always fuck things up, you probably either avoid opportunities (so you don't fuck them up) or you unconsciously sabotage them when they're going well (because success doesn't fit your narrative). Either way, things don't work out. See? You always fuck things up.

The narrative becomes reality. Not because it was true to begin with, but because believing it made it true.

This is simultaneously depressing and empowering. Depressing because you've been creating your own suffering through your stories. Empowering because if you created it, you can change it.

Creating Your Preferred Story

Narrative therapists talk about "preferred stories." These are versions of your narrative that reflect your values and possibilities rather than just your wounds and limitations.

This isn't fantasy. It's not pretending you have powers you don't have or denying difficulties you've faced. It's telling the most complete, most empowering version of your actual story.

Here's how to craft one:

Acknowledge what happened. Don't erase the hard parts. They're part of your story.

Identify what you learned. What strengths did you develop? What insights did you gain? How did you grow?

Recognize your agency. Where did you make choices, even constrained choices? Where did you influence outcomes, even partially?

Connect to your values. What matters to you? How does your story reflect those values? How can moving forward align with them?

Leave room for possibility. Your story isn't finished. The ending isn't written. What becomes possible when you're not limited by your old narrative?

Example:

Old story: "I'm broken from childhood trauma. I'm damaged. I'll never be whole."

Preferred story: "I survived difficult circumstances that could have destroyed me. I'm still healing. I've developed resilience, empathy, and strength through confronting what happened. I'm not defined by what was done to me but by how I've chosen to respond. I'm worthy of connection, love, and healing. My past is part of my story, not the totality of it. I'm still becoming."

Both versions acknowledge trauma. One version traps you. The other frees you.

You Are the Author

Here's the most important thing about narratives. You're telling them. You're the author.

Not the only author but circumstances, other people, and systems all shape your story too. But you're the one interpreting events, assigning meaning, deciding what counts as significant, choosing what to emphasize and what to minimize.

Authorship means you have power to revise.

The story you've been telling about yourself and the world isn't handed down from the universe as objective truth. It's a interpretation you've been constructing, often unconsciously, based on selective evidence and inherited frameworks.

You can construct differently.

Not by lying. Not by denying reality. But by choosing more complete, more accurate, more empowering interpretations of the same facts.

Your current narrative isn't serving you. It's keeping you stuck in doom loops, confirming your worst beliefs, limiting your possibilities.

Time to write a different story.

Same protagonist. Different interpretation. Better ending.

You're not fucked. You've just been telling yourself you are.

Revise the narrative.

Watch what becomes possible.

12

The Practice of Presence

I missed my kid's first words because I was checking X. Not metaphorically. Literally. My partner said, "Did you hear that?" I looked up from my phone, confused. "Hear what?" Our kid had just said their first recognizable word, and I was three feet away, physically present but mentally somewhere else entirely, scrolling through strangers' opinions about something I can't even remember now.

I was there, but I wasn't there.

This is the defining experience of modern life: being physically present while mentally absent. We're at dinner with friends but checking email. Playing with our kids but planning tomorrow. Having sex but thinking about work. In conversations but composing our next text.

We're living everywhere except where we actually are.

And the cost is staggering. We're missing our own lives! Not dramatically, not all at once, but moment by moment, distraction by distraction, until we look back and realize we were barely present for any of it.

The Cost of Chronic Absence

Here's what living in constant distraction steals from you:

Your experiences. You can't fully experience something you're not paying attention to. That concert, meal, sunset, or conversation, they happened. But you weren't really there for them. You have memories of checking your phone during them, but not of the experiences themselves.

Your relationships. Being with someone who's physically present but mentally elsewhere is lonely. And you're doing it to everyone in your life while also being upset when they do it to you. Real intimacy requires presence not just proximity.

Your rest. You can't actually rest if your mind is always churning through the past or racing into the future. Your body might be still, but your nervous system is activated. You're exhausted but never refreshed.

Your peace. Most anxiety lives in the future (catastrophizing about what might happen) or the past (ruminating about what did happen). When you return to the present moment, the catastrophe usually isn't actually happening right now. The danger is imagined, not real.

Your life itself. This is the big one! You only ever live in the present moment. The past is memory. The future is imagination. This moment, right now, is the only time you're actually alive. If you're never present for it, you're not really living. You're just thinking about living.

Why Presence Is So Hard

Let's be honest: you already know you should be more present. You've heard it before. You've probably tried and failed. Here's why it's genuinely difficult:

Your brain is literally being trained toward distraction. Every notification, every context switch, every bit of multitasking rewires your brain for fragmented attention. You're not weak-willed but you're up against sophisticated technology designed to keep you distracted.

Presence isn't always pleasant. Sometimes the present moment contains discomfort, boredom, or pain. Your mind escapes into past or future because now is difficult. This is protective, but it's also how you never develop capacity to be with difficulty.

The culture rewards busyness over presence. Multitasking is praised. "Productivity" means doing multiple things simultaneously. Taking time to just be present feels like wasting time that could be spent producing.

You've practiced absence far more than presence. You've spent thousands of hours training distraction. Presence is a skill that requires practice to develop. Of course it's hard! You're trying to reverse years of conditioning.

What Mindfulness Actually Is

Strip away the mysticism and the wellness industry branding, and mindfulness is simple: paying attention to your present-moment experience on purpose, without judgment.

That's it. Not enlightenment. Not spiritual awakening. Just training your attention to stay with what's actually happening right now instead of constantly wandering into past or future.

It's not about:

- Stopping thoughts (impossible)
- Achieving blissed-out peace (nice when it happens, not the goal)
- Being spiritual or religious (can be, doesn't have to be)
- Sitting cross-legged for hours (helpful for some, not required)

It's about:

- Noticing where your attention is
- Redirecting it when it wanders
- Being with your actual experience instead of lost in narrative about it
- Developing the skill of present-moment awareness

Think of it as mental training, like going to the gym for your attention.

Basic Practices: Start Here

Breath awareness (5 minutes): Sit comfortably. Notice your breath! Feel it most clearly (chest, belly, nostrils). Count breaths if helpful: in (one), out (one), in (two), out (two), up to ten, then start over. When your mind wanders (it will, constantly), notice without judgment and return to the breath. That's the practice: wandering and returning, over and over.

Body scan (10 minutes): Lie down or sit. Bring attention to your feet. Notice any sensations like pressure, temperature, tingling, numbness. Move attention slowly up through your body: ankles, calves, knees, thighs, hips, belly, chest, hands, arms, shoulders, neck, face, head. Just noticing, not trying to change anything.

Mindful observation (3 minutes): Choose an object. Really look at it. Notice colors, textures, shapes, shadows, details you normally miss. When your mind starts narrating or judging, return to pure observation. You're not thinking about the object. You're seeing it!

Informal mindfulness: Do any routine activity (washing dishes, brushing teeth, walking) with full attention. Notice sensations, movements, sounds. When your mind wanders to planning or remembering, return to the activity. This turns ordinary moments into practice.

Common Obstacles and Misconceptions

"I can't stop my thoughts." You're not supposed to. Thoughts will happen. The practice is noticing them and returning attention to the present, not eliminating them.

"I'm bad at this." There's no "good" or "bad" at mindfulness. If you noticed your mind wandered and returned attention to the present, you did it correctly. That's the practice.

"I don't have time." Five minutes counts. One mindful breath counts. You don't need hour-long sessions. Brief, regular practice is more effective than occasional marathon sessions.

"My mind is too busy/anxious/ADHD for this." Busy, anxious, or ADHD minds often benefit most from mindfulness practice. It's harder, yes. That's why it's valuable. Start very small, be patient, consider guided recordings.

"I fell asleep." That's rest, which you apparently needed. Not mindfulness, but not a failure either. Try practicing sitting up or at a different time of day.

"Nothing happened." Something always happens. You're just expecting fireworks. The benefit is cumulative and subtle, not dramatic and immediate.

Presence in Relationships

The greatest gift you can give another person is your full attention. Not your divided attention while you scroll. Not your partial presence while you plan your response. Your full, undivided, present attention.

When someone is talking to you, actually listen. Not just to respond, not to fix, not to judge—to understand. Notice their words, tone, body language. Be with them in that moment.

This is rare enough to be revolutionary. Most people are so unused to being fully attended to that genuine presence feels profound.

And here's what it does for you: it deepens your relationships exponentially. Presence creates intimacy. Absence creates loneliness even when you're together.

Plus, practicing presence with others trains presence generally. The skill transfers.

Presence with Difficult Emotions

Here's something counterintuitive: being present with difficult emotions often makes them less overwhelming, not more.

When you're anxious and you try to escape it (distraction, suppression, avoidance), the anxiety intensifies. Your avoidance signals to your brain that the feeling is dangerous, which increases anxiety.

When you're present with anxiety—"I'm noticing anxiety in my chest, tightness in my throat, racing thoughts"—you're observing it rather than being consumed by it. There's a subtle but crucial difference between "I am anxious" and "I'm noticing anxiety."

The first one, you're merged with the emotion. The second one, you're witnessing it. That witness position creates space.

Same with pain, anger, sadness. You don't have to like these feelings. You just have to stop running from them. When you stop running and turn to face them, they often lose some of their power.

This doesn't mean toxic positivity or spiritual bypassing. It means developing capacity to be with difficulty without being destroyed by it.

Presence and Worry

Most worry is time travel.

You're replaying the past (rumination) or rehearsing catastrophic futures (anxiety). In either case, you're not actually in the present moment.

Here's a powerful practice: When you notice yourself worrying, ask: "Am I okay right now, in this exact moment?"

Not "Will I be okay tomorrow?" Not "Was I okay yesterday?" Right now, this breath, this moment.

Usually, the answer is yes. The catastrophe isn't happening now. It's imagined. The danger is in your thoughts about future or past, not in present reality.

This doesn't solve the actual problems you're worried about. But it reveals that right now, in this breath, you're okay. And right now is the only time you're ever actually living.

From that place of present-moment okayness, you can address future concerns more effectively than from a place of catastrophic anxiety.

Cultivating Presence in Daily Life

Digital boundaries: No phones for the first and last 30 minutes of the day. No screens during meals. Phone in another room when having conversations. These create spaces for presence.

Single-tasking: Do one thing at a time. Not email while on a call. Not social media while watching TV. One thing, full attention. This feels weird initially. Do it anyway.

Intentional transitions: Between activities, pause. Take three breaths. Consciously shift attention from the last thing to the next thing. Don't just race from task to task on autopilot.

Presence check-ins: Set random reminders (several times a day): "Where is my attention right now?" Notice. If it's not where you want it, redirect. This builds the habit of awareness.

Mindful moments: Designate certain routine activities as mindfulness practice. Every time you wash your hands, be fully present for it. Every time you walk through a doorway, notice. Small anchors throughout the day.

Presence partnerships: Agree with someone to gently point out when you're not present with them. "You're on your phone." This creates accountability and awareness.

Presence Is Life

Here's the bottom line: your life is not something that will happen someday when conditions are right. Your life is happening right now.

Every moment you're mentally absent is a moment you're not actually living. You're existing, yes. Surviving, sure. But not fully living.

The past is gone. The future isn't here. This moment, right **NOW**, is all you ever have. If you're never present for it, you're missing everything.

Not because you're lazy or broken or doing it wrong. Because you're human in a culture designed to fragment your attention and keep you distracted from your own experience.

Presence is the practice of reclaiming your life from that fragmentation.

It doesn't require perfection. It doesn't require hours of meditation.

It doesn't require becoming someone you're not.

It just requires noticing when you're absent and choosing to return. Over and over. Moment by moment.

That's it. That's the practice.

And it might be the most important practice in this entire book.

Because you can have all the purpose, connection, resilience, and optimism in the world, but if you're never actually present to experience them, what's the point?

Be here.

Now.

This is your life.

Don't miss it.

13

Embracing Uncertainty

I used to think the opposite of anxiety was calm. Turns out, the opposite of anxiety is tolerance for uncertainty.

For years, I tried to eliminate uncertainty from my life. I researched every decision to death. I made contingency plans for my contingency plans. I tried to predict every possible outcome and prepare for all of them. I consumed news obsessively, convinced that if I just knew enough, I could anticipate what was coming and protect myself from it.

This strategy had one major flaw. It didn't work.

The more I tried to eliminate uncertainty, the more anxious I became. Because uncertainty is fundamental to existence and trying to eliminate it is like trying to eliminate weather. You can prepare for rain, but you can't make it never rain. You can only make yourself miserable trying.

The shift came when I realized the question wasn't "How do I make everything certain?" It was "How do I function, even thrive, when nothing is certain?"

Completely different question. Completely different life.

Why We Crave Certainty

Your brain is a prediction machine. It's constantly trying to forecast what will happen next so it can prepare appropriate responses. This worked great when the variables were limited: which berries are safe, where predators hide, how the seasons work.

But now you're trying to predict variables like global pandemics, economic systems, technological disruption, climate change, political chaos, and whether your text message came across as passive-aggressive.

Your prediction machine is overloaded, and it's freaking out.

Uncertainty registers in your brain as threat. When you don't know what's going to happen, your nervous system activates as if danger is present. Not-knowing feels dangerous because, evolutionarily, not-knowing often was dangerous.

This is why we'll sometimes choose a negative certainty over an uncertain possibility. Better to know for sure that something bad will happen than to live in the anxiety of maybe. At least if you know the bad thing is coming, you can stop waiting for the other shoe to drop.

This is also why uncertainty has gotten so much harder recently. The world has genuinely become more unpredictable. Climate patterns are shifting. Economic systems are volatile. Technology is disrupting faster than we can adapt. Political norms that seemed stable have collapsed. The rules we thought governed reality keep changing.

Your brain's certainty-craving isn't irrational. It's just trying to survive in a world that's become genuinely harder to predict.

How We Try (And Fail) to Eliminate Uncertainty

Watch what you do when uncertainty spikes:

Obsessive information consumption. You scroll news, check updates, refresh feeds, consume analysis. If you just know enough, maybe you can predict what's coming. Except information doesn't eliminate uncertainty but often increases it by exposing you to more variables and conflicting interpretations.

Rigid control. You micromanage, over-plan, try to dictate outcomes.

If you can just control everything, maybe you can prevent bad things. Except most things aren't actually in your control, and trying to control the uncontrollable just exhausts you.

Decision paralysis. You can't choose because you don't know which choice is "right." So you don't choose, which is still choosing. You're just choosing to let circumstances decide for you.

Excessive planning. You make detailed plans for every scenario, trying to prepare for all possibilities. This feels productive but is often procrastination disguised as preparation. You're planning instead of acting.

Denial or magical thinking. You pretend uncertainty doesn't exist, convince yourself you know how things will turn out, or engage in superstitious thinking to create illusion of control.

None of these eliminate uncertainty. They just burn your energy trying to make the unmakeable certain.

Uncertainty Tolerance: A Learnable Skill

Here's the good news: your capacity to handle uncertainty isn't fixed. It's a skill you can develop.

Uncertainty tolerance is the ability to remain functional, and even creative, when you don't know what will happen. It's not eliminating the discomfort of not-knowing; it's increasing your capacity to feel that discomfort without being controlled by it.

Like building physical strength, you build uncertainty tolerance gradually through practice:

Start small. Practice sitting with minor uncertainties before tackling major ones. Order something new at a restaurant without researching it first. Take a different route without GPS. Make a small decision quickly without extensive analysis. Notice the discomfort, breathe through it, see that you survive.

Notice your physical experience of uncertainty. Where do you feel it in your body? Chest tightness? Stomach clenching? Jaw tension?

Just notice without trying to fix. The sensation itself isn't dangerous but it's damn uncomfortable.

Practice the phrase "I don't know, and that's okay." When you don't know something, instead of scrambling to find out or pretending you do know, practice saying this. Out loud or internally. "I don't know what will happen. I don't know if this will work. I don't know if I'm making the right choice. And that's okay."

Distinguish between productive and unproductive uncertainty responses. Productive: gathering relevant information, making the best decision you can with available information, preparing for likely scenarios. Unproductive: obsessive information consumption, trying to prepare for every possible scenario, paralysis.

Reflect on past uncertainties you survived. You've been uncertain before. Many times. And you're still here. You navigated not-knowing then. You can navigate it now.

Uncertainty as Source of Possibility

Here's the reframe that changes everything: uncertainty isn't just threat. It's also possibility.

If outcomes were certain, nothing new could emerge. No change would be possible. Everything would be predetermined. Your actions wouldn't matter because the future would be fixed.

Uncertainty means outcomes aren't predetermined. Which means your actions could influence them. Which means possibility exists.

Think about it: every positive surprise in your life happened because the future was uncertain. Every unexpected joy or lucky break that turned out better than expected, those exist because outcomes weren't fixed.

If you could eliminate uncertainty, you'd eliminate possibility too. You'd get predictability, but you'd lose potential.

The uncertain future might contain difficulties. It also might contain opportunities, solutions, positive developments you can't currently imagine. You don't know. That's the point. And in that not-knowing, there's room for things to be different than you expect, including better.

Uncertainty and Realistic Optimism

Remember realistic optimism from Chapter 5? It doesn't require certainty. In fact, it depends on uncertainty.

We can't be certain things will work out. But we also can't be certain they won't. The future is genuinely open.

Given that openness, we have a choice: assume the worst and give up, or assume our efforts might matter and engage.

Neither assumption is more "realistic." Both are guesses about an unknowable future. But one assumption keeps you engaged and creative. The other paralyzes you.

Realistic optimism says: "I don't know if this will work. I'm going to try anyway, because trying keeps options open that despair closes."

This isn't denial of uncertainty. It's action in the face of uncertainty. It's refusing to let not-knowing become a reason for not-doing.

Decision-Making Under Uncertainty

Uncertainty makes decisions hard. Here's how to decide anyway:

Accept "good enough." You'll rarely have perfect information. Make the best decision you can with what you know, then commit. Waiting for certainty often means never deciding.

Distinguish reversible from irreversible decisions. Reversible decisions (trying a new job, moving to a new city) can be changed if they don't work out. Make these faster. Irreversible decisions (having a child, major surgery) deserve more deliberation. But even these can't wait for perfect certainty.

Focus on next steps, not final outcomes. You don't need to know how the entire path unfolds. You just need to know the next step. Take it. Then assess and choose the next step from there.

Build in flexibility. Instead of rigid plans that assume you know how things will go, create flexible approaches that can adapt as situations change. Prepare to adjust rather than trying to predict everything.

Set decision deadlines. "I'll decide by Friday" prevents endless dithering. You gather information until the deadline, then you decide with what you have.

Practice deciding with 70% information. If you wait until you have 100% certainty, you'll never decide. Research suggests 70% is often the sweet spot. Enough information to make a reasonable choice without paralysis.

Specific Uncertainty Manifestations

Decision paralysis: Set a timer. 10 minutes to gather information, then decide. Use a coin flip if you're truly torn between equal options. Often your reaction to the coin's result tells you what you actually want.

Worst-case scenario thinking: Ask yourself: "What's the worst that could realistically happen? Could I handle it?" Usually yes. Then: "What's the best that could happen? What's the most likely outcome?" Get the full range, not just catastrophic possibilities.

Excessive planning: Set a planning time limit. One hour to plan, then execute. Planning beyond a certain point is just anxiety displacement.

Inability to commit: Recognize that not committing is also a choice with consequences. Sometimes the cost of keeping all options open is higher than the cost of choosing one.

The Paradox of Acceptance

Here's what's wild: accepting uncertainty actually reduces your suffering from it.

When you fight uncertainty, you're fighting reality. That fight is exhausting and futile. The uncertainty still exists, plus now you're exhausted from fighting it.

When you accept uncertainty like "I don't know what will happen, and I'm okay with not knowing", then you stop fighting. The uncertainty still exists, but you're not adding suffering to it by struggling against it.

It's the difference between being in turbulent water while fighting the waves (you're struggling and drowning) versus being in turbulent water while relaxing and floating (still turbulent, but you're conserving energy and staying afloat).

This doesn't mean you like uncertainty or that it doesn't affect you. It means you stop pretending you can eliminate it and start learning to navigate within it.

Surfing vs. Controlling the Ocean

You can't control the ocean. You can't make the waves stop. You can't make the water calm because you want it calm.

You can learn to surf.

You can develop balance, timing, and skill at riding waves. You can get better at reading patterns. You can build strength and flexibility to handle turbulence.

But you can't make the ocean stand still.

This is true for uncertainty too. You can't make life predictable. You can't eliminate not-knowing. You can't force outcomes to be certain.

You can develop the capacity to function gracefully within uncertainty. You can get better at making decisions with incomplete information. You can build resilience for when things don't go as planned. You can learn to find possibility in the unpredictable.

The ocean will keep moving. Waves will keep coming. Storms will happen.

You can keep trying to make it stop and staying miserable.

Or you can learn to surf and find freedom in the movement.

Living in the Uncertain

Every major decision you'll make involves uncertainty. Who to partner with, what career to pursue, where to live, whether to have children, how to spend your limited time, none of these come with guarantees.

You could wait for certainty. You'll wait forever.

Or you can accept that uncertainty is the medium of existence and learn to move within it.

Not recklessly though, you still gather information, consider consequences, make thoughtful choices. But without the illusion that enough thinking will make outcomes certain.

The future is unknown. It always has been. It always will be.

You can make that fact a source of perpetual anxiety, or you can make it a source of freedom.

Nothing is predetermined. Outcomes aren't fixed. Your actions matter because the future is still being written.

That's terrifying. It's also liberating.

You don't know what will happen.

Neither does anyone else.

Welcome to being human.

Now make your choice anyway.

14

Media Literacy for Sanity

I used to pride myself on being well-informed. I read multiple news sources daily, followed breaking developments in real-time, and could discuss current events in detail. I felt like a responsible citizen staying engaged with the world. This was even after I left journalism.

I was also having constant low-grade panic attacks.

The breaking point came when I realized I could tell you intricate details about political scandals in countries I'd never visited, celebrity drama I didn't care about, and crises I had zero ability to influence. But I couldn't tell you the last time I'd had a genuine conversation with my neighbor.

I wasn't well-informed. I was well-agitated. There's a difference.

Modern media literacy isn't just about identifying fake news or checking sources. It's about recognizing how media is designed to manipulate your attention and emotions, understanding the business models that profit from your anxiety, and developing the skills to consume information without being consumed by it.

This isn't optional anymore. Your mental health depends on it.

The Business Model That's Breaking Your Brain

Let's start with the uncomfortable truth: most media isn't designed to inform you. It's designed to keep you engaged so you can be shown advertisements.

Engagement = eyeballs = money.

And what drives engagement better than anything? Emotional arousal. Fear, outrage, anxiety, anger! These keep you clicking, scrolling, sharing. Calm, nuanced information that helps you understand complex issues? That's boring. You might read it once and move on. Can't monetize that.

So the system optimizes for what keeps you hooked:

Breaking news (constant urgency, never time to process)

Conflict (choose your side, get angry at the other side)

Outrage bait (look at this terrible thing someone said/did)

Catastrophizing (everything is a crisis)

Personalization (turn systemic issues into individual villains)

Novelty over importance (shocking beats significant)

This isn't conspiracy theory. It's just capitalism. Media companies aren't evil; they're businesses responding to economic incentives. But those incentives align with keeping you anxious, not keeping you informed.

Understanding this changes how you consume. You stop taking the presentation at face value and start asking: "Why am I being shown this? What emotion is this designed to trigger? Who benefits from me feeling this way?"

News vs. Analysis vs. Opinion

Most people can't distinguish between these three, which is a massive problem:

News is reporting of verifiable events: "The bill passed 52-48." "Three inches of rain fell." "The company announced layoffs." Facts that can be confirmed.

Analysis is interpretation of events: "This bill will likely affect small businesses by..." "The rain patterns suggest..." Expert perspective that helps you understand significance.

Opinion is someone's personal viewpoint: "This bill is a disaster." "We should be outraged about..." Someone's feelings or beliefs about events.

The problem is that modern media blurs these constantly. Opinion pieces are presented as news. Analysis contains embedded opinions. News is framed to suggest particular interpretations.

You end up consuming opinions and analysis while thinking you're consuming news. Then you're confused and anxious because you can't distinguish between "this happened" and "this is what someone thinks about what happened."

Practice this: When consuming media, identify which category you're reading. Is this reporting facts, analyzing implications, or expressing opinions? Once you start looking, you'll be shocked how much "news" is actually opinion.

The Confirmation Bias Trap

Here's how your media diet probably works:

You have existing beliefs. Algorithms notice what you engage with. They show you more content that confirms those beliefs. You engage with it (of course because it agrees with you!). The algorithm concludes you want more of this and shows you more extreme versions. Your beliefs become more rigid and extreme. You're now in an echo chamber that feels like reality.

This happens to everyone, regardless of political affiliation or intelligence. It's not a personal failing. It's just how recommendation algorithms work.

The result is you're consuming a carefully curated slice of reality optimized to make you feel like everyone agrees with you (if you're in a confirmation bubble) or everyone is crazy (if you're hate-reading the other side). Neither is true. You're just in a filter bubble.

Breaking out requires deliberate effort:

Follow people who challenge your thinking. Not trolls, but thoughtful people with different perspectives. This is uncomfortable. Do it anyway.

Seek out primary sources. Instead of reading what people say about a report/study/speech, find and read the actual report/study/speech. You'll be surprised how often the reporting misrepresents it.

Diversify your sources. If you only read sources that lean one direction, you're getting a skewed picture. Read across the spectrum, then synthesize.

Notice your emotional reactions. When something makes you feel strongly (outraged, vindicated, smug), that's a sign to be extra careful. Strong emotion suggests you're being manipulated or having biases triggered.

Identifying Manipulation Techniques

Media uses specific techniques to manipulate your perception. Learn to spot them:

Selective framing: Using true facts but choosing which facts to emphasize to create a particular impression. "Crime up 2% this year" vs. "Crime down 40% over past decade." Both can be true, creating opposite impressions.

Emotional language: Using charged words instead of neutral ones. "Slammed," "destroyed," "controversial," "shocking." These words trigger emotions rather than convey information.

False equivalence: Presenting two sides as equally valid when they're not. "Some scientists say climate change is real, others disagree" implies equal evidence when consensus is overwhelming.

Cherry-picking: Highlighting examples that support the narrative while ignoring contradictory data. "Look at this one person who had a bad outcome with X" while ignoring thousands who didn't.

Manufactured urgency: Making everything "breaking news" to trigger stress response and keep you engaged. Most breaking news doesn't actually require immediate awareness.

Decontextualization: Removing context that would change inter-pretation. A quote taken out of context, a statistic without comparison points, an event without historical background.

When you spot these, you're seeing manipulation, not information.

The Outrage Economy

Outrage is addictive. It gives you:

- Moral clarity (we're good, they're bad)
- Community (bonding over shared anger)
- Purpose (we must fight this!)
- Dopamine (righteous anger feels good)

Media knows this. So they feed you outrage constantly. Something to be angry about every single day. Someone who said something terrible. Someone doing something unacceptable. Someone you should be furious at.

And here's the thing: some outrage is justified. Real injustices exist. But when you're perpetually outraged about everything, you become:

Exhausted (constant anger depletes you)

Ineffective (diffuse outrage doesn't translate to focused action)

Manipulated (your outrage is being monetized)

Desensitized (everything is outrageous, so nothing is)

Ask yourself: "Is this outrage serving me or the algorithm? Is it motivating constructive action or just burning my energy?"

If it's the latter, disengage.

Fact-Checking Without Losing Your Mind

You should verify information before sharing or believing it. But you can't fact-check everything. No, you'd never do anything else.

Here's a practical approach:

For claims that trigger strong emotion: Pause before sharing.

Check it. Strong emotion suggests potential manipulation.

For surprising claims: If it seems too perfectly aligned with your beliefs or too outrageous to be true, verify it. Confirmation bias and outrage bait both thrive on unchecked sharing.

Use reliable fact-checking sites: Snopes, FactCheck.org, PolitiFact, your local newspaper's fact-check column. Not perfect, but better than random social media.

Check the source: Who published this? What's their track record? What's their business model or bias? This doesn't make them wrong, but it provides context.

Look for primary sources: Don't just read what someone says about a study. Go and find the actual study. Don't just read someone's interpretation of what someone said. But find the actual quote in context.

Be willing to update beliefs: If fact-checking reveals you were wrong, update your understanding. Clinging to disproven beliefs because you already shared them is ego, not integrity.

Building a Healthier Media Diet

Think nutrition: mostly whole foods, some processed foods, minimal junk food.

Whole food information: Long-form journalism, books, primary sources, in-depth reporting. Requires effort to digest but actually nourishes understanding.

Processed food information: Curated newsletters, reputable news summaries, aggregated sources. More convenient than whole food, less nutritious but not harmful in moderation.

Junk food information: Outrage bait, hot takes, social media rage-scrolling, clickbait, breaking news addiction. Engineered for maximum palatability and minimum nutrition. Terrible as primary diet.

Most people are living on information junk food and wondering why they feel sick.

Practical guidelines:

Set specific times for news consumption (twice daily, 20 minutes max). Outside those times, news is closed.

Unsubscribe from sources that consistently leave you agitated without actually informing you.

Replace breaking news with weekly summaries. Most "breaking" news isn't information you need immediately.

Choose depth over breadth. Better to deeply understand three issues than to shallowly track thirty.

Balance problem-focused news with solution-focused journalism. If you only read about what's broken, you'll think nothing works.

Digital Hygiene Practices

Use tools to limit exposure:

- Browser extensions that block news sites during certain hours
- Apps that limit social media time
- News aggregators that let you choose topics rather than algorithm-fed doom

Curate ruthlessly:

- Unfollow accounts that consistently spike your anxiety
- Mute keywords that trigger you
- Block bad-faith actors instead of engaging
- Remember: your timeline should serve you, not stress you

Create friction for bad habits:

- Delete apps from phone (can still access via browser, but added friction helps)
- Log out after each use

- Turn off all notifications except essential ones
- Put time limits on high-risk apps

Build better defaults:

- Replace news-checking with reading something substantive
- Replace social media scrolling with actual connecting
- Replace opinion consumption with primary source reading

When to Completely Disconnect

Sometimes the best media literacy practice is consuming no media at all.

Take regular information fasts: 24 hours, a weekend, a week. Notice what happens:

You don't actually miss anything crucial. Genuine emergencies reach you through other means. Everything else can wait.

Your nervous system calms. The constant stimulation and outrage aren't agitating you.

You have mental space for deeper thinking. Your mind isn't fragmented by information snacking.

You're more present with your actual life. Instead of consuming other people's experiences, you're having your own.

Try this monthly. It recalibrates your relationship with information and reminds you that being constantly "informed" isn't actually necessary or healthy.

The Goal Isn't Perfect Information But Functional Understanding

You will never be perfectly informed about everything. That's not the goal. The goal is:

Understanding enough to make good decisions in areas that affect you directly.

Having enough context to see through obvious manipulation.

Maintaining the mental health and energy needed to engage meaningfully with what actually matters.

Not being consumed by information designed to consume you.

You don't need to know everything. You need to know how to evaluate what you encounter, when to dig deeper, when to let go, and how to protect your attention and wellbeing from systems designed to exploit them.

That's media literacy for sanity.

Not perfect knowledge. Just functional bullshit detection and healthy boundaries around information consumption.

In a world drowning in information designed to manipulate you, that might be the most important skill you can develop.

15

Rest as Resistance

I used to wear my exhaustion like a badge of honor.

Five hours of sleep? That's dedication. Working through weekends? That's commitment. Skipping meals and vacation days? That's hustle. I was productive, busy, important! All the things our culture celebrates.

I was also falling apart. Constantly sick, emotionally volatile, unable to focus, running on fumes and calling it ambition.

The moment everything shifted was when someone said to me: "Your exhaustion serves the system that's exploiting you. Your rest is an act of resistance."

I got defensive immediately. Rest wasn't resistance! It was laziness, indulgence, something you earned after you'd accomplished enough. Rest was what weak people needed. Strong people pushed through.

That narrative, I now realize, is exactly what keeps us productive and depleted, generating value for others while destroying ourselves.

Rest isn't weakness. In a culture that profits from your exhaustion, rest is revolution.

The Culture of Exhaustion

We live in a system that treats rest as suspicious.

If you're not constantly busy, you must not be important. If you're sleeping eight hours, you must not be ambitious. If you're taking time off, you must not be serious about success. The person who brags about their 80-hour workweek gets admiration. The person who maintains boundaries gets quietly judged.

This isn't an accident. Capitalism requires productivity. The more hours you work, the more value you generate for others. Your exhaustion is profitable—for your employer, for the economy, for anyone who benefits from your output.

Your wellbeing, on the other hand, doesn't show up in GDP. Your rest doesn't generate quarterly returns. Your health has no stock price.

So the culture conditions you to feel guilty about rest, to see it as laziness rather than necessity, to believe that constant productivity is virtue and self-care is selfish.

We've internalized the idea that our worth is measured by our output. Rest produces nothing. Therefore rest makes us worthless.

This is propaganda, and it's killing us.

The Research: Rest Isn't Optional

Let's talk about what actually happens when you don't rest:

Sleep deprivation impairs cognitive function more than alcohol. At 17-19 hours without sleep, you're performing at the level of someone with a blood alcohol content of 0.05%. Miss enough sleep regularly and you're essentially operating drunk.

Chronic stress from insufficient rest leads to cardiovascular disease, weakened immune function, inflammation, accelerated aging, and increased risk of basically every major health problem.

Decision-making ability plummets when you're exhausted. The same brain that makes good choices when rested makes catastrophically bad ones when depleted.

Emotional regulation requires rest. Without it, you become reactive, volatile, unable to handle normal stressors. Your relationships suffer. Your mental health deteriorates.

141

Creativity and problem-solving happen during rest, not during constant grinding. Your brain consolidates learning, makes novel connections, and solves problems in the background while you're resting. Deprive yourself of rest and you're not just tired, you're stupid. This isn't self-help fluff. This is biology. Your body and brain require rest to function. Trying to operate without adequate rest is like trying to drive a car without oil. You might manage for a while, but you're causing damage that will eventually become catastrophic.

Types of Rest You Need

Rest isn't just sleep, though sleep is foundational. You need multiple types:

Physical rest: Sleep, obviously. But also: lying down when you're tired, taking naps if you can, reducing physical demands when your body needs recovery. Your body is not an infinite resource.

Mental rest: Breaks from cognitive work. Your brain can't run at full capacity indefinitely. Even short breaks improve performance and prevent burnout. Pomodoro technique exists for a reason.

Sensory rest: Reducing stimulation from screens, noise, lights, crowds. Constant sensory input is exhausting. You need quiet, darkness, stillness to let your nervous system settle.

Social rest: Time alone if you're overstimulated by people, or quality time with people who energize rather than drain you if you're isolated. This varies by personality, but everyone needs some version of restorative social experience.

Creative rest: Experiencing beauty without producing anything. Nature, art, music are what fill you up rather than deplete. Not "productive" creativity, just receptive appreciation.

Emotional rest: Permission to feel what you feel without having to perform or manage others' emotions. Space to process without judgment.

Most people are deficient in multiple types. You might be sleeping adequately but never getting mental rest. Or getting physical rest but living in constant sensory overload. Rest needs to be comprehensive.

Rest as Strategic, Not Selfish

Here's the reframe that helps if you're struggling with guilt:

Rest isn't opposed to productivity, in fact, it enables productivity. You're not less effective when you rest appropriately; you're more effective. Well-rested you makes better decisions, thinks more creatively, works more efficiently, and sustains effort longer.

Elite athletes know this. They train hard, yes. They also prioritize rest and recovery because that's when adaptation happens, when the body gets stronger. Nobody accuses Olympic athletes of being lazy for sleeping nine hours or taking rest days.

Your brain and body work the same way. You can't grow stronger, smarter, or more capable without adequate rest. Rest isn't time stolen from achievement, instead it's investment in capacity.

If you won't rest for yourself, rest strategically. Rest because it makes you more effective at whatever you're trying to accomplish. Rest because depleted you can't do the work that rested you could do.

This isn't the best reason to rest. You deserve rest regardless of productivity. But if productivity is your current metric, at least understand that rest serves that metric too.

The Guilt Problem

The biggest obstacle to rest isn't time but guilt.

You feel guilty resting when:

- Other people are working
- There's more to be done (there's always more)
- You haven't "earned" it yet
- The world is on fire and you're taking a nap
- Rest feels like giving up

This guilt is conditioned. You were taught that your worth depends on your productivity, so anything that reduces productivity feels like moral failure.

But here's the truth: Your worth is inherent. It doesn't depend on your output. You don't have to earn the right to rest. You're not a machine that needs to justify maintenance.

As for the world being on fire, yes, there are problems. There will always be problems. You address them better when you're rested than when you're depleted. Martyring yourself doesn't help anyone. It just creates one more problem: you, broken and useless.

The guilt is a control mechanism. It keeps you productive for others while destroying yourself. Recognize it as such and reject it.

Practical Rest in an Exhausting World

Protect your sleep. Non-negotiable. Whatever it takes: dark room, white noise, temperature control, consistent schedule, no screens before bed. Eight hours isn't lazy but minimum maintenance.

Build in micro-rest. If you can't take big chunks, take small ones. Five-minute breaks between tasks. Ten minutes of sitting still at lunch. Brief walks. These accumulate.

Create rest rituals. Signals to your nervous system that it's safe to rest. Evening routine, weekend mornings, whatever tells your body "you can stand down now."

Say no more. Every yes to something is a no to rest. Protect rest by protecting your time. This means disappointing people sometimes. They'll survive. You might not if you keep this up.

Disconnect regularly. Phone off. Email closed. True unavailability, not performative unavailability where you're still checking "just in case."

Notice early warning signs. Irritability, difficulty concentrating, getting sick frequently, emotional volatility, needing coffee to function, all of these are your body screaming for rest. Listen before it forces you to listen through breakdown.

Take actual days off. Not working from home days. Not catching up on email days. Actual rest days where you do not work. Revolutionary concept, apparently.

Rest Inequity

I need to acknowledge that rest is a privilege not everyone has access to:

Economic pressure means some people work multiple jobs to survive. They're not choosing exhaustion. It's being forced on them.

Caregiving responsibilities mean some people, especially women, never stop working. Paid work ends, unpaid work begins.

Systemic barriers mean rest is harder for people dealing with poverty, discrimination, unsafe living conditions, or lack of support systems.

This isn't individual failing but a structural problem. Individual rest practices help but don't solve systemic rest deprivation.

We need both: personal practices to reclaim what rest we can, and collective action to change systems that make rest impossible for too many people.

If you have access to rest and aren't taking it, you're squandering a privilege others desperately need. If you don't have access to rest, the problem isn't your time management but systemic injustice that needs addressing.

When You Physically Can't Rest

Sometimes rest feels impossible because:

Your nervous system is stuck in activation. Trauma, chronic stress, or anxiety can make it physically difficult to rest even when you try. This might need professional support with therapy or possibly medication.

Your circumstances are genuinely relentless. Young kids, caregiving, financial pressure, crisis. Sometimes you're in a season where adequate rest isn't possible. This is real. Survive it, seek support where you can, and know it won't be forever.

You've forgotten how. Years of hustle culture have trained you to be uncomfortable with stillness. Rest feels like failure, like you're wasting time. This requires practice. Start small. Build tolerance for non-productivity.

If rest feels impossible, you probably need it most. Find whatever tiny bits you can. Five minutes counts. One adequate night of sleep counts. Anything that moves you from total depletion toward slightly less depletion.

Rest as Resistance

Here's why rest is revolutionary:

It refuses the narrative that your worth equals your productivity. When you rest, you're claiming value independent of output. You're saying "I matter whether I'm producing or not."

It rejects exploitation. Systems profit from your exhaustion. Your rest denies them that profit. It's reclaiming your time, your body, your life for yourself.

It models alternatives. In a culture of hustle, your rest gives others permission to rest. You're not just changing your life but you're also challenging the culture.

It maintains your capacity for sustained resistance. You can't fight systemic problems if you're too depleted to function. Rest isn't checking out. It's maintaining the strength needed for continued engagement.

It prioritizes long-term sustainability over short-term productivity. The system wants you to burn bright and burn out. Rest is choosing to burn steadily instead.

Every time you rest when the culture tells you to hustle, you're committing a small act of rebellion. You're saying: "My humanity is more important than my productivity. My wellbeing is non-negotiable.

I will not destroy myself for systems that don't value me."

That's resistance.

Permission

You don't need to earn rest. You don't need to wait until everything is done (it never is). You don't need to prove you're tired enough (you are). You don't need permission from anyone.

But since we've all been so thoroughly conditioned to need permission, here it is:

You are allowed to rest.

You are allowed to sleep eight hours. To take days off. To do nothing. To lie in the sun. To nap. To turn off your phone. To disappoint people who expect constant availability. To prioritize your wellbeing over their convenience.

You are allowed to be a human being with a body that requires rest, not a machine that should run indefinitely.

Your rest is not selfish. It's not lazy. It's not giving up.

It's maintenance. It's resistance. It's reclaiming your humanity from systems that want to treat you as a resource to be extracted.

Rest.

Not because you've earned it, but because you're alive and alive things need rest.

Rest because you're fighting a long battle and you need your strength.

Rest because your exhaustion serves systems that don't serve you.

Rest because it's the most revolutionary thing you can do in a culture that profits from your depletion.

Rest. Now.

16

Community as Infrastructure

When the pandemic hit, I learned exactly how isolated I'd become. I lived in a neighborhood for three years and couldn't name five neighbors. I had colleagues but not friends. I had hundreds of online connections but no one to call when I needed help. I'd built my life around independence and self-sufficiency, proud that I didn't need anyone.

Then suddenly I couldn't get groceries or toilet paper, and couldn't handle being alone indefinitely. And I had no community infrastructure to fall back on because I'd never built any.

I watched people in strong communities organize mutual aid, share resources, check on vulnerable neighbors, create support systems. Meanwhile, I was alone, ordering everything online, having no one and being no one to anyone.

That's when I understood that individualism isn't strength. It's fragility disguised as independence.

Real resilience comes from community. And community isn't something that just happens but it's infrastructure you build, maintain, and invest in before you need it.

Why We've Lost Community

Let's acknowledge what happened:

Suburban sprawl designed environments where you need a car to go anywhere, making casual encounters rare. No walking to corner stores, no sidewalk conversations, no third places where community naturally forms.

Economic pressure requires longer hours, longer commutes, less time and energy for community participation. You're too exhausted from work to show up for anything else.

Digital displacement created the illusion of connection while eroding actual community. You're scrolling through strangers' lives instead of engaging with your neighbors.

Cultural individualism sold us the myth that needing people is weakness, that self-sufficiency is the highest virtue, that "I did it myself" is something to aspire to rather than a sign of privilege or loneliness.

Mobility means people move frequently for jobs, education, opportunities. Harder to invest in community when you might leave in two years.

Decline of traditional institutions like churches, civic organizations, unions, whatever you think of them politically, they provided community infrastructure that's largely gone now.

The result is record levels of loneliness, isolation, and fragility. We're nominally independent but actually helpless when crisis hits because we have no one to fall back on.

Community as Resilience

Here's what research shows about communities with strong social capital:

Better health outcomes. People in connected communities live longer, recover from illness faster, and have lower rates of depression and chronic disease. Connection is literally medicine.

Economic opportunity. Jobs, resources, information, and support flow through networks. Strong communities create economic resilience for their members.

Effective crisis response. When disaster hits, connected communities mobilize faster and more effectively than isolated individuals waiting for institutional response.

Higher life satisfaction. Belonging to community predicts happiness better than income, education, or most other factors.

Collective efficacy. Communities can accomplish things individuals can't. Organize for change, improve neighborhoods, solve local problems, protect vulnerable members.

This isn't romantic nostalgia. It's measurable reality. Communities aren't nice-to-have. They're infrastructure for human wellbeing and survival.

What Community Actually Means

Community is an overused word that's lost meaning. Let's be specific:

Geographic community: People who live near you. Neighbors, local businesses, neighborhood organizations. Proximity creates opportunities for casual connection and mutual support.

Identity community: People who share aspects of identity like culture, ethnicity, sexuality, disability, profession. Provides belonging, understanding, shared experience.

Interest community: People who share passions, hobbies, or pursuits. Book clubs, sports teams, maker spaces, advocacy groups. Common interests create bonds.

Chosen family: People you're deeply connected to regardless of blood relation or proximity. Your ride-or-die people, your emergency contacts, your found family.

Online community: Digital spaces of connection around shared interests or experiences. They're real but limited and can't bring you soup when you're sick or help you move.

You need some combination. Relying on one type leaves gaps. Geographic community for daily life, identity community for belonging,

COMMUNITY AS INFRASTRUCTURE

interest community for meaning, chosen family for depth, online community for reach.

Building Community Where You Are

You can't manufacture instant deep community, but you can create conditions where it develops:

Start with proximity. Introduce yourself to neighbors. Learn names. Have brief pleasant interactions. You're building familiarity, which is prerequisite for trust.

Show up repeatedly. Join something that meets regularly. Community requires repeated casual contact over time. Attend the neighborhood meeting, join the running club, volunteer at the food bank. Consistency matters more than intensity.

Be the initiator. Someone has to suggest coffee, organize the gathering, and start the group chat. Be that person. Yes, you risk rejection or having nobody show up. Do it anyway. Most people want connection but are waiting for someone else to make the first move.

Offer specific help. Not "let me know if you need anything" (they won't tell you). "I'm going to the store, can I grab you anything?" "I'm making extra soup, want some?" "I have Thursday free, need help with that project?" Specific offers are easier to accept.

Accept help offered. When someone offers, say yes. Let people contribute. Giving people opportunity to help builds bonds and creates reciprocity.

Create rituals. Weekly coffee, monthly potluck, annual block party. Rituals signal that community matters enough to prioritize regularly.

Use your specific resources. Maybe you have a truck people can borrow. A yard for gatherings. Skills you can share. A network you can connect people to. Tools you can lend. Contribute what you uniquely have.

The Vulnerability of Community

Community requires something modern culture teaches us to avoid:

interdependence.

You have to admit you need people. You have to let people see your struggles. You have to ask for help. You have to be willing to owe people and be owed. You have to trust that reciprocity will balance over time even when it's not equal in every moment.

This is terrifying if you've been taught that independence is strength.

But here's the reality: we're already interdependent. You depend on people for food, electricity, water, roads, internet, basically everything. The myth of independence is just that, a myth. You're already relying on massive systems of interdependence, just impersonal ones.

Community is choosing visible, personal interdependence over invisible, systemic dependence. It's saying: "I'd rather depend on people I know who depend on me than on faceless systems that don't care about me."

This requires vulnerability. And vulnerability requires courage.

But the alternative, the isolation of false independence, is more fragile than any community interdependence.

Different Ways to Contribute

Not everyone contributes the same way. Community needs variety:

Organizers: People who make things happen, coordinate, plan, follow through. Communities need organizers.

Connectors: People who know everyone and introduce people to each other. Social glue. Communities need connectors.

Resources: People who have specific skills, tools, knowledge, or access they can share. Communities need resources.

Care: People who check in, notice who's struggling, provide emotional support. Communities need care.

Consistency: People who just reliably show up. Not flashy, just present. Communities need consistency.

Specialists: People with niche skills that are occasionally crucial like legal knowledge, medical training, carpentry, whatever. Communities need specialists.

You don't have to be everything. Figure out what you're good at or positioned to offer and contribute that. Let others fill other roles.

Navigating Community Challenges

Community isn't utopia. It's people, which means complexity:

Conflict happens. You won't agree with everyone. You won't like everyone. Community doesn't mean forced harmony. It means learning to work with people despite differences.

Boundaries matter. Community doesn't mean total availability or losing yourself. You can be part of community while maintaining limits on your time and energy.

Power dynamics exist. Race, class, gender, ability, and age all affect who has voice and influence. Good community acknowledges and actively addresses power imbalances.

Burnout is real. A few people often do most of the work. Prevent this by: rotating responsibilities, acknowledging contributions, saying no sometimes, building sustainable rather than heroic practices.

Not everyone reciprocates. Some people take more than they give. This is okay to some extent because community means supporting people through different seasons. But chronic one-sidedness needs addressing.

Exclusion can happen. Communities can become cliques. Intentionally welcome newcomers, create onramps for entry, notice who's on the margins.

These challenges don't mean community is impossible but it requires intention, communication, and work.

Online Community: Benefits and Limits

Digital community is real community for some purposes:

Finding rare connections. If you're dealing with unusual circumstances, have niche interests, or belong to small identity groups, online community might be your only option for finding others like you.

Maintaining distant relationships. Staying connected with people you can't see regularly. Digital tools can enhance geographic community even when they can't replace it.

Learning and resource-sharing. Access to knowledge, resources, and support from people across distance.

But digital community has limits:

It can't meet physical needs. Can't bring you soup, help you move, give you a hug, watch your kids, lend you a tool.

It's easier to ghost. Low commitment means people disappear when it's inconvenient. Less accountability than face-to-face community.

It can become substitute. Using online connection to avoid local connection leaves you digitally connected but practically isolated.

Use digital community to supplement, not replace, physical community. They serve different needs.

Starting Where You Are

You don't need to build massive community infrastructure overnight. Start small:

This week: Introduce yourself to one neighbor. Learn their name. Have a brief pleasant interaction.

This month: Attend one local thing like a meeting, event, group, whatever. Just show up.

This quarter: Join something that meets regularly. Commit to going consistently for three months.

This year: Organize one gathering. Invite neighbors for coffee, start a book club, host a potluck, whatever. Small is fine.

Each small action builds infrastructure. You're creating familiarity, trust, reciprocity, and relationships. This accumulates over time into actual community.

Community as Politics

Strong communities aren't just nice, they're political.

Communities resist exploitation. When people support each other, they're less vulnerable to predatory systems. Mutual aid reduces dependence on exploitative employers, landlords, or institutions.

Communities build power. Organized people can make demands, protect members, change policies, shift resources. Isolated individuals can't.

Communities model alternatives. When communities successfully meet needs outside capitalist markets, they prove different ways of organizing are possible.

Communities protect vulnerable members. Collective care beats individual struggle. Communities can shield people from systemic violence that individuals face alone.

Building community is collective resistance to systems that profit from isolation.

The Infrastructure You Need

You know how physical infrastructure like roads, bridges, water systems need to be built before crisis hits? Same with community.

You can't build community when you need it. You build it before you need it, maintain it consistently, and then it's there when crisis comes. This means:

- Investing time in relationships before you need help
- Contributing to community before you need support
- Building trust gradually over repeated interactions
- Showing up even when it's inconvenient
- Treating community as essential infrastructure, not optional extra

Community isn't what you do after you've handled everything else. It's foundational infrastructure that makes everything else possible.

You Are Necessary

Here's what individualism gets wrong: you're not a burden on community. You're necessary to it.

Community needs your participation, your skills, your presence, your perspective. You're not taking from community by being part of it but creating it through participation.

Your vulnerability creates space for others' vulnerability. Your needs give others opportunity to contribute. Your presence makes the community stronger, richer, more resilient.

You don't have to earn belonging. You belong because you're there.

Show up. Contribute what you can. Accept help when offered. Be part of something larger than yourself.

That's how we survive. That's how we thrive. That's how we build the infrastructure we need for the world we're living in.

Not alone. Together.

Build community.

Your survival—all our survival—depends on it.

17

Your Personal Sustainability Plan

I've lost count of how many times I've done this!

Get inspired by a book, podcast, or revelation. Decide to completely overhaul my life. Create an elaborate plan involving waking up at 5 AM, meditating for an hour, journaling, exercising, eating perfectly, reading, learning languages, and becoming a completely different person.

Last exactly four days. Maybe a week if I'm really committed.

Crash spectacularly. Feel like a failure. Conclude that I'm just not disciplined enough, motivated enough, or good enough to maintain positive change.

Return to old patterns, now with bonus shame and self-loathing.

This cycle repeated so many times I started believing I was fundamentally incapable of sustained change. I could sprint, but I couldn't maintain. I could have bursts of excellence, but I couldn't sustain them.

The problem wasn't discipline or willpower. The problem was treating change like a sprint when it's actually a marathon. Or, more accurately, treating it like a temporary intervention when it needs to be sustainable integration.

This chapter is about building practices that last. Not perfect practices. Not heroic practices. Just sustainable ones.

The Boom-Bust Cycle

Here's the pattern most people follow:

Inspiration phase: Something clicks. You see the problem clearly. You're motivated to change. Everything seems possible.

Intense effort phase: You go all-in. Maximum effort, dramatic changes, complete commitment. You're doing *All The Things*. You feel amazing.

Depletion phase: The intensity isn't sustainable. You're exhausted. Life happens. The perfect system cracks.

Collapse phase: You can't maintain it, so you abandon it completely. All or nothing thinking means if you can't do it perfectly, you don't do it at all.

Shame phase: You feel like a failure. Conclude you lack discipline. Internalize that you're just not capable of sustained change.

Return to baseline phase: Back to old patterns, now with additional shame.

Repeat: Next inspiration starts the cycle again.

This isn't personal failure. This is predictable outcome of unsustainable approach.

What Makes Practices Sustainable

Small enough to do on bad days. If your practice requires peak motivation and perfect conditions, it's not sustainable. Sustainable practice is what you can maintain when you're tired, stressed, or dealing with life chaos.

Aligned with your actual values, not aspirational ones. You should do this because it actually matters to you, not because you think it should matter or because someone else values it.

Simple systems, not willpower. Willpower is finite and unreliable. Systems like habit stacking and accountability structures work when willpower doesn't.

Built-in flexibility. Life changes. Circumstances shift. Sustainable practices can adapt rather than shattering when conditions aren't perfect.

Actually enjoyable, or at least tolerable. If you hate it, you won't sustain it. Find versions of beneficial practices that don't make you miserable.

Integrated, not added. Building on existing routines works better than creating entirely new ones. Attach new practices to existing anchors.

Minimum Viable Practice

This concept changed everything for me:

Instead of "I'm going to meditate for an hour daily," try "I'm going to take three conscious breaths before starting work."

Instead of "I'm going to exercise for 90 minutes six days a week," try "I'm going to move my body for 10 minutes daily."

Instead of "I'm going to write 2000 words every morning," try "I'm going to write one sentence."

These aren't your goals. They're your *minimums*. The baseline you maintain even on terrible days. The floor, not the ceiling.

Here's the magic: once you've done the minimum, you often do more. Three conscious breaths becomes five minutes of meditation. Ten minutes of movement becomes a full workout. One sentence becomes a paragraph.

But even when you just do the minimum, you've maintained the practice. You've built the habit. You've stayed consistent.

Consistency at a lower level beats perfection you can't maintain.

Energy Accounting

You have finite energy. Treating it like an infinite resource guarantees burnout.

Energy in:

- Adequate sleep

- Nutritious food
- Movement
- Rest and recovery
- Joy and play
- Connection and belonging
- Purpose and meaning
- Beauty and inspiration

Energy out:

- Work (paid and unpaid)
- Relationships (maintaining, deepening, navigating)
- Life maintenance (cleaning, cooking, errands, admin)
- Emotional labor (processing feelings, managing stress, supporting others)
- Decision-making
- Context switching and interruptions
- Dealing with systems (bureaucracy, healthcare, etc.)

Your sustainability plan needs to balance this equation. If energy out consistently exceeds energy in, you're running a deficit that will eventually bankrupt you.

Track for a week: What actually energizes you versus what depletes you? Where are you leaking energy unnecessarily? What could you eliminate, delegate, or reduce?

Building Your Personal Plan

Audit current reality: What's actually working? What's not? Where are you depleted? Where do you have energy? What practices have you maintained (even imperfectly)? What have you repeatedly tried and failed at?

Identify core values: What actually matters to you? Your practices should serve these.

Choose 3-5 foundational practices: Not 20. Not 50. Three to five practices that would most impact your wellbeing and resilience. For most people, this includes: adequate sleep, some form of movement, some form of connection, some form of presence/mindfulness, and some form of meaning/purpose engagement.

Define minimum viable versions: What's the smallest version of each practice you could maintain even on terrible days? That's your baseline.

Create systems, not reliance on motivation:

- Environmental design (make good choices easier, bad choices harder)
- Habit stacking (attach new practice to existing routine)
- Accountability (someone checks in, or you track publicly)
- Removal of friction (prepare ahead, eliminate obstacles)
- Identity alignment ("I'm someone who..." rather than "I'm trying to...")

Build in flexibility: What happens when life disrupts your plan? Have backup versions. "If I can't do X, I'll do Y." You're not abandoning practice but adapting it.

Schedule regular review: Monthly check-in: Is this still working? What needs adjustment? Are you maintaining or depleting? Practices that worked in one season might not work in another. Adjust accordingly.

Seasons and Cycles

You're not a machine. Your capacity varies by:

- Season of life (raising young kids vs. empty nest vs. retirement)
- Literal season (winter affects energy differently than summer)

- Health status (chronic illness, recovery, aging all affect capacity)
- Circumstances (crisis, stability, transition all require different approaches)
- Cycles (menstrual, circadian, whatever rhythms affect you)

Stop expecting consistency across these variables. Your practice should have seasons too.

Winter practice might look different than summer practice. Crisis mode looks different than stability mode. High-energy periods can sustain more than low-energy periods.

This isn't failure. It's adaptation. Sustainable practice adapts to reality rather than demanding reality adapt to it.

Dealing with Perfectionism

Perfectionism is the enemy of sustainability.

Perfectionism says: Do it perfectly or don't do it at all. All or nothing. If you miss once, you've failed, so quit.

Sustainability says: Do what you can with what you have. Something is better than nothing. Missing once means you start again, not that you've failed.

Practice this shift:

- From "I ruined my streak" to "I'm starting again"
- From "I should do X" to "I choose to do X" or "I'm not doing X right now"
- From "I failed" to "I learned something about my capacity and will adjust"
- From "This isn't working" to "This isn't working yet in this form. How can I adapt it?"

Perfectionism keeps you trapped in boom-bust cycles. Sustainability builds over time through imperfect consistency.

When to Add, When to Subtract
You don't need to keep adding practices indefinitely. Sometimes sustainability requires subtraction.
Add when:

- You've maintained current practices consistently for at least a month
- You have capacity and energy for more
- You've identified a clear gap or need
- The addition serves your actual values

Subtract when:

- You're maintaining practices out of guilt rather than value
- Something isn't serving you anymore
- Your life circumstances have changed
- You're depleted and need to conserve energy
- You're doing it because you think you should rather than because it matters

Sustainability sometimes means doing less, not more. Protecting capacity by releasing what's not essential.
Accountability Without Shame
External accountability helps, but it can also create shame and pressure that undermines sustainability.
Helpful accountability:

- Someone who checks in with curiosity, not judgment
- Tracking that shows patterns without moral weight
- Community that celebrates showing up, not just succeeding
- Structures that make follow-through easier

Unhelpful accountability:

- Someone who shames you for missing
- Tracking that becomes obsessive or anxiety-inducing
- Competition that makes it about performance
- Structures that create additional stress

Choose accountability that supports sustainability, not that creates additional pressure.
Your Sustainability Worksheet
Current state:

- What's working right now?
- What's not working?
- Where am I depleted?
- Where do I have energy?

Core values:

- What actually matters to me?
- What do I want my life oriented toward?

Foundation practices (3-5):

1. [Practice] - Minimum version: [what you can do on worst days]
2. [Practice] - Minimum version:
3. [Practice] - Minimum version:

Systems and support:

- How will I make these easier to do?

- What obstacles need removing?
- Who/what will help me stay consistent?

Flexibility plan:

- When circumstances change, what's my backup version?
- How will I adapt rather than abandon?

Review schedule:

- When will I check in and adjust?
- What will I look for in my review?

The Long Game

Here's what sustainable practice looks like over time:

Week 1: Excited, doing minimums and probably more. Everything feels possible.

Month 1: Some days you do minimums. Some days you do more. Some days you miss. You keep starting again.

Month 3: Practice is becoming automatic. You don't think about it as much. You just do it. Mostly.

Month 6: You've adapted the practice several times to fit changing circumstances. It looks different than when you started. That's good.

Year 1: This is just what you do now. Not perfectly. Not every day without fail. But consistently enough that it's integrated into your life.

Year 5: You can't imagine not having this practice. It's sustained you through multiple life changes, adapted to different seasons, weathered various challenges.

That's sustainability. Not perfection. Not even consistency in the rigid sense. But practices that flex with life while remaining present.

You Don't Need Heroic Discipline

The goal isn't becoming someone with superhuman willpower who can maintain perfect practices indefinitely.

The goal is building systems and practices that work for who you actually are, with the actual capacity you actually have, in the actual life you're actually living.

This requires:

- Honesty about your limits
- Willingness to start small
- Patience with the process
- Flexibility to adapt
- Self-compassion when you stumble
- Commitment to starting again rather than quitting

You're not building a perfect system. You're building a sustainable one.

And sustainable means it can last. Through changes, challenges, setbacks, and seasons.

Not because you're disciplined enough to maintain it.

But because you built it to be maintainable.

That's how change sticks.

Not through heroic effort you can't sustain.

But through small practices you can maintain.

Build for sustainability.

Start now.

18

When Things Still Feel Fucked

Let's be honest. You can do everything in this book and still have days, weeks, maybe months when everything feels completely fucked.

You can practice gratitude and still feel hopeless. You can build community and still feel lonely. You can embrace uncertainty and still be paralyzed by anxiety. You can take meaningful action and still feel like nothing matters. You can rest and still be exhausted.

This isn't failure. This is being human in a genuinely difficult world.

I need to address this directly because self-help books often end with the implicit promise: "Do these things and you'll be fine." And then when you do these things and you're not fine, you conclude you did them wrong, or you're broken, or the whole thing was bullshit.

None of those are true.

The practices in this book work. They're backed by research and lived experience. But they're not magic spells that eliminate suffering. They're tools that help you navigate difficulty—and sometimes difficulty is just really fucking difficult regardless of tools.

What This Book Can and Can't Do

What these practices can do:

- Reduce the frequency and intensity of despair
- Give you more good days and fewer terrible ones
- Build resilience so struggles don't destroy you
- Provide frameworks for making sense of chaos
- Connect you to resources (internal and external) for coping
- Help you find meaning and purpose even in hard times

What these practices cannot do:

- Eliminate all pain, anxiety, or despair
- Make genuinely difficult circumstances magically easy
- Cure mental health conditions that require professional treatment
- Solve systemic problems you're affected by
- Guarantee that everything will work out fine
- Make you permanently "fixed" or immune to struggle

If you're still struggling after implementing these practices, that doesn't mean you failed. It might mean you need additional support, or that you're dealing with genuinely overwhelming circumstances, or simply that you're human and humans struggle sometimes.

When Practices Stop Working

Sometimes practices that worked become ineffective:

You've hit your current capacity. The practices helped you reach a new baseline, but you've hit the limit of what individual practices can address. You might need professional support, medication, therapy, or systemic changes.

Your circumstances have changed. Practices that worked in stability don't work in crisis. Practices that worked when you had support don't work in isolation. You're not doing them wrong. The context has shifted.

You've been going through the motions. You're doing the practices mechanically without actual engagement. This happens. Sometimes you need to refresh your approach or take a break and come back.

The practices never actually fit you. Not everything works for everyone. Maybe you need different practices, or different versions of these practices, or a completely different approach.

You're dealing with something that requires more than self-help. Clinical depression, trauma, severe anxiety, and grief are real conditions that often need professional intervention, not just personal practices.

If practices stop working, don't assume you're doing them wrong. Assess honestly: Is this a capacity issue? A context issue? An engagement issue? A fit issue? A "need professional help" issue?

Troubleshooting Common Problems

"I'm doing everything right but still feeling terrible."

First: Are you actually doing them, or going through motions? There's a difference between practicing gratitude by genuinely noticing what sustains you versus mechanically listing three things before bed.

Second: "Everything" might be too much. Maybe you're over-efforting at practices and that itself is depleting you.

Third: Feeling terrible despite practices might mean you need support beyond practices. That's okay. That's not failure.

"I fell off track and now I can't start again."

You're experiencing the perfectionism trap. You think: "I broke the streak, so I failed, so why bother?" This is a thought, not a truth.

Start again. Right now. You don't need to wait for Monday or January 1st or when conditions are perfect. Just start again from wherever you are.

"Nothing helps."

If genuinely nothing helps, you might be dealing with clinical depression or another condition that needs medical intervention. Please talk to a professional.

169

If some things help a little but not enough, that's different. That's not "nothing helps"—that's "I need more or different support."

"I'm doing worse since I started."

Sometimes awareness of problems makes them feel worse before they feel better. You're noticing things you were numbing yourself to.

But if you're genuinely worse, stop the practices that aren't serving you and consider professional support.

"I don't have the energy/time/resources for this."

Then your practice needs to be: survive. That's it. Survival is enough. When you have more capacity, you can add more. For now, just survive.

When Professional Help Is Needed

Self-help books are not substitutes for mental healthcare. You might need professional support if:

Symptoms persist despite effort:

- Persistent depression lasting weeks or months
- Anxiety that interferes with daily functioning
- Intrusive thoughts you can't control
- Suicidal ideation (if you're thinking about suicide, please call 988 or go to an emergency room)

Trauma is affecting you:

- Flashbacks, nightmares, hypervigilance
- Inability to feel safe
- Dissociation or feeling disconnected from yourself
- Past trauma interfering with present life

Your functioning is seriously impaired:

- Can't work or maintain relationships

- Struggling with basic self-care
- Substance use to cope
- Behaviors that harm you or others

You've tried and can't do this alone:

- Practices feel impossible to implement
- You need accountability and guidance
- Your support system isn't enough

Seeking help isn't admitting defeat. It's recognizing that some things require professional expertise. You'd see a doctor for a broken leg. Mental health deserves the same respect.

Different Types of Hard

Temporary hard: Acute crisis, major life transition, grief, specific challenge. This will pass. Practices help you survive until it does.

Chronic hard: Ongoing difficult circumstances that won't change soon such as poverty, caregiving, chronic illness, discrimination. Practices help you survive within it, but they don't fix the circumstances. Systemic change is also needed.

Neurochemical hard: Depression, anxiety disorders, ADHD, trauma responses are brain chemistry issues that may need medication alongside practices. Not moral failing, not lack of trying hard enough. Medical conditions.

Existential hard: The fundamental uncertainty and difficulty of being human in a chaotic universe. This never fully resolves. Practices help you make meaning within it.

Different types of hard require different responses. Know which you're dealing with.

Both/And Thinking for Hard Times

When things feel fucked, practice holding multiple truths simultaneously:

- This is really hard AND I'm handling it
- I'm struggling AND I'm not broken
- I can't fix this AND I'm not powerless
- This sucks AND it won't last forever
- I need help AND asking for help is strength
- Things are bad AND they're not only bad
- I'm in pain AND pain is not permanent
- I feel hopeless today AND feelings shift
- This seems impossible AND I've survived impossible before

Not either/or. Both/and.

Emergency Protocols

When you're in acute distress and need immediate relief:

For panic/anxiety:

- Box breathing: in for 4, hold for 4, out for 4, hold for 4
- 5-4-3-2-1 grounding: name 5 things you see, 4 you hear, 3 you feel, 2 you smell, 1 you taste
- Cold water on face or ice in hands
- Call someone safe

For despair/depression:

- Get outside, even briefly
- Move your body, even just walking in place
- Eat something, drink water
- Reach out to one person, even just a text
- Do one tiny thing that usually brings comfort

For overwhelm:

- List what's in your control right now (probably very little)
- Choose one thing from that list
- Do just that one thing
- Ignore everything else temporarily

For numbness/dissociation:

- Physical sensation: splash face, stretch, pressure on body
- Name where you are out loud
- Describe your surroundings in detail
- Do something that requires focus (puzzle, game, task)

These aren't solutions. They're stabilization. Get stable first, then address underlying issues.

Redefining "Better"

"Better" doesn't mean perfect, fixed, or permanently happy.

Better might mean:

- Having more okay days than terrible days
- Struggling but recovering faster
- Asking for help instead of suffering alone
- Noticing small good things even when much is bad
- Functioning even when you don't feel good
- Surviving hard things without being destroyed
- Finding moments of peace within chaos
- Feeling connected even when struggling

Raise your definition of "better" from "everything is fine" to "I'm surviving and occasionally thriving despite genuine difficulty."

Permission to Not Be Okay

You're allowed to not be okay.

You're allowed to struggle despite doing "everything right." You're allowed to feel despair even though there's also beauty. You're allowed to be angry, scared, exhausted, or overwhelmed.

Positive practices don't mean positive feelings all the time. They mean you have tools for navigating the full range of human experience, including the really hard parts.

Don't add suffering to suffering by believing you shouldn't be suffering.

You're human. Humans struggle. That's reality.

Collective Crisis

Sometimes things feel fucked because things genuinely are fucked on a collective level:

Climate crisis, political instability, economic inequality, social breakdown, ongoing injustice are so very real. Your individual practices can help you cope with them, but they can't single-handedly fix systemic problems.

Your individual despair might be appropriate response to collective crisis. Don't pathologize your reaction to genuinely fucked-up circumstances.

And: you still need to function, find meaning, connect with others, and take care of yourself even while acknowledging that things are collectively difficult. Both/and, not either/or.

19

What Helps When Nothing Seems to Help

Lower the bar. Maybe the goal isn't thriving. Maybe it's just surviving today. That's enough.

Return to basics. Sleep, food, water, safety, connection. When everything is overwhelming, focus on fundamental needs.

Take the smallest possible step. Not a big intervention. Not a dramatic change. Just one tiny thing that's slightly less terrible than doing nothing.

Let someone help you. Even if it's just sitting with you. Even if it's just listening. Even if they can't fix anything.

Remember this is temporary. Feelings shift. Circumstances change. This exact configuration of difficulty won't last forever.

Give yourself permission to just survive. You don't have to be optimizing, improving, growing, or achieving. Survival is enough.

Starting Again (And Again)

You'll fall off track. You'll stop practicing. You'll return to old patterns. You'll struggle despite knowing better.

This is normal. This is the process.

The practice isn't never falling. It's getting back up. Starting again. Not from where you wish you were, but from where you actually are.

Every moment is an opportunity to start again:

- This breath
- This hour
- This day
- Right now

You don't need to wait for perfect conditions. You don't need to feel motivated. You just need to start again from wherever you are, however many times it takes.

Still Here

If you're reading this chapter, you're still here.

You've survived every difficult day so far. That's not nothing. That's actually extraordinary.

The practices in this book are tools. Some will work for you. Some won't. Some will work for a while and then stop. Some will work differently than expected.

That's okay. You're not failing. You're living.

And living means sometimes struggling, sometimes thriving, sometimes barely surviving, and sometimes not knowing which one you're doing.

All of that is okay.

All of that is human.

You're not fucked.

You're just here, doing your best with what you have, trying to navigate genuinely difficult circumstances with imperfect tools and finite resources.

That's enough.

You're enough.

Even on the days when it doesn't feel like it.

Especially on those days.

Keep going.

20

The Practice Continues

Here we are at the end, which is really just a beginning.

You've spent nineteen chapters learning about your brain's architecture, examining narratives, building resilience, reclaiming attention, practicing presence, and constructing the infrastructure for a life that doesn't feel completely fucked. You know more now than you did when you started. You have tools, frameworks, practices, perspectives.

And maybe you're wondering: Now what?

Because knowing is different from doing, and doing once is different from sustaining, and sustaining requires something that books can't give you, which is the actual daily practice of living with intention in a world that makes intention difficult.

So let me tell you what happens next, as honestly as I can.

What Integration Actually Looks Like

You're not going to implement everything in this book. You're probably not going to implement most of it. You'll read some chapters that resonate deeply and others that feel irrelevant or inaccessible. You'll try some practices that stick and others that don't. You'll have insights that shift your perspective immediately and others that take months or years to truly understand.

This is exactly how it's supposed to work.

The point was never to become a person who perfectly executes all twenty chapters' worth of guidance. The point was to find the specific pieces that address your specific struggles in your specific circumstances, and to practice those pieces in ways that actually fit your life.

Maybe for you, it's Chapter Four on reclaiming attention. You needed permission to step back from the doomscroll and concrete strategies for doing so. Maybe it's Chapter Nine on connection. You've been isolated and needed to see that community is infrastructure you can build. Maybe it's Chapter Sixteen on rest as resistance. You needed someone to tell you that your exhaustion serves systems that don't serve you.

Whatever resonated, start there. Not with everything. Not with perfection. Just start with the piece that calls to you most strongly and see what happens when you practice it.

The Non-Linear Path

I want to set realistic expectations about what practice looks like over time, because every self-help book makes it sound like linear progress: you start here, you work through the steps, you arrive there, transformed and thriving.

That's not how it works.

Real practice looks like this: you have a breakthrough, then you forget everything and revert to old patterns. You build a sustainable routine, then life disrupts it and you don't practice for weeks. You feel genuinely better, then something happens and you're back in the despair you thought you'd moved past. You integrate a practice deeply, then discover it needs to evolve because you've changed or your circumstances have changed.

This isn't failure. This is the actual shape of growth.

You're not climbing a mountain with a clear peak where you plant a flag and declare yourself done. You're navigating terrain that keeps shifting, learning to adapt as you go, developing skills that deepen and change over time. Sometimes you move forward. Sometimes you move sideways. Sometimes you circle back to territory you thought you'd already covered, only to discover you're seeing it differently now.

The practice isn't reaching some final destination of "fixed" or "healed" or "optimized." The practice is engaging, again and again, with whatever your current reality requires.

When You Forget Everything

You will forget what you learned here. Not permanently, but temporarily. You'll have a crisis and all these frameworks will evaporate from your mind. You'll slide back into doomscrolling, catastrophizing, isolation, exhaustion, despair. You'll lose the thread entirely.

This has happened to me countless times with practices I theoretically know work. I'll be doing great, maintaining practices, feeling resilient, and then some combination of stress and circumstances will hit and suddenly I'm back to baseline dysfunction like I never learned anything.

When this happens—not if, when—here's what to remember: The practice isn't never forgetting. The practice is remembering again. It's coming back to what you know works, even after you've forgotten it for a while. It's having the resources to return to, even when you've temporarily abandoned them.

Each time you return, you're strengthening that return pathway. You're building the skill of recovery, of starting again, of remembering what helps. This itself is practice, maybe the most important one.

You don't need to remember everything all the time. You just need to remember enough, eventually, to find your way back when you've wandered off.

The Practices That Stick

Over time, you'll notice that some practices naturally integrate while others remain effortful. The ones that integrate are probably the ones that genuinely fit your wiring, your values, your life. They stop feeling like practices and start feeling like just how you operate now.

This might be a gratitude practice that's become automatic. You notice good things without trying because you've trained that attention. It might be presence practices that mean you're naturally more aware of when you're mentally absent. It might be boundary-setting around media consumption that's now just how you structure your days. It might be community participation that's become essential to your life rather than something you have to remember to do.

Let these practices solidify. Don't feel obligated to keep efforting at practices that never quite fit. Some practices are right for certain seasons and not others. Some practices work for other people but not for you. That's fine. Keep what serves you, release what doesn't, stay open to revisiting practices later when circumstances change.

The goal isn't collecting the most practices. It's finding the specific practices that help you live the specific life you want to live.

Sharing What You Learn

As you practice, you'll probably notice yourself naturally sharing what's helping you. You'll tell a friend about the attention audit. You'll recommend the uncertainty tolerance exercises. You'll talk about rest as resistance or community as infrastructure. You'll find yourself explaining concepts from this book in your own words, contextualized to your experience.

This is good. This is how these practices spread and evolve. Every person who finds something useful and shares it with someone else is creating ripples that extend beyond their individual benefit.

But here's what I want you to watch out for: the temptation to become evangelical about practices that worked for you. Just because something transformed your life doesn't mean it's the answer for everyone. Just because gratitude practice saved you from despair doesn't mean the person who says it feels fake or forced is doing it wrong.

Share what helped you, absolutely. But hold it lightly. Offer it as one option among many, not as the solution everyone must adopt. Listen to how others are navigating similar struggles in different ways. Learn from their practices too.

The conversation is richer when we're all bringing our different experiences and discoveries rather than insisting everyone follow the same prescription.

The Ongoing Uncertainty

Nothing in this book eliminates uncertainty about the future. The world is still chaotic. Climate change is still real. Political instability continues. Economic systems remain volatile. Injustice persists. Your personal struggles don't magically disappear because you've developed better frameworks for understanding them.

What changes is your relationship to that uncertainty. You're not trying to eliminate it anymore. You're developing capacity to navigate within it. You're not waiting for the world to become stable before you can be okay but you're building resilience that works within instability.

This is uncomfortable, because it means releasing the fantasy that if you just do enough personal growth work, everything will become secure and certain. It won't. Uncertainty is permanent. Difficulty is ongoing. The practices don't make those realities disappear.

What they do is help you engage with those realities without being destroyed by them. They help you find meaning, connection, purpose, and even joy within circumstances that remain genuinely challenging. They help you contribute to making things better without requiring certainty that your contributions will be enough.

You're learning to surf, not to still the ocean. The ocean will keep moving. And you'll keep surfing.

Building on What's Here

This book is not the final word on any of this. It's one perspective, one set of frameworks, one collection of practices drawn from research, experience, and synthesis. But there are other perspectives, other frameworks, other practices that might serve you better or differently. Keep learning. Keep exploring. Keep finding what works for you. Read other books. Try other approaches. Talk to other people navigating similar challenges. Build on what's here rather than treating it as complete or definitive.

And as you practice, you'll develop your own insights, your own variations, your own wisdom. You'll figure out what I got wrong for you specifically. You'll discover nuances and applications I didn't think of. You'll adapt practices to fit your unique circumstances in ways no general book could prescribe.

That's exactly what should happen. You're not trying to become a faithful practitioner of someone else's system. You're taking useful tools and building your own approach to living well in difficult times.

When You Help Someone Else

At some point, you'll encounter someone drowning in the same doom spiral you've navigated. They'll be convinced everything is fucked, that nothing they do matters, that the world is ending and they're powerless to change any of it. And you'll recognize that state because you've been there.

You might share what helped you. You might just sit with them in it. You might offer resources or perspective or simply presence. Whatever you do, you'll be contributing to their navigation of difficulty, the way others contributed to yours by writing books or sharing practices or just being there when you needed them.

This is how these practices spread and sustain. Not through perfect implementation, but through imperfect humans helping other imperfect humans navigate shared struggles. Not through expertise, but through solidarity. Not through having all the answers, but through offering what helped us while acknowledging it might not be what helps them.

Every person who moves from drowning in despair to swimming with difficulty is someone who can then help the next person. Not because they're fixed or healed or enlightened, but because they learned to swim and remember what drowning felt like.

You're part of that chain now. Imperfectly. Incompletely. But genuinely.

The Practice Never Ends

Here's what I need you to understand about the title of this chapter: the practice continues because the practice never concludes.

There's no graduation from being human in a difficult world. There's no moment where you've done enough work that you're permanently fixed. There's no final achievement of optimism or resilience or presence that means you never struggle again.

The practice is ongoing because life is ongoing. You don't practice presence until you've mastered it and then stop. You practice presence continually because presence is how you engage with ongoing life. You don't build resilience until you're resilient enough and then coast. You keep building it because challenges keep coming.

This might sound exhausting! That the work is never done! But it's actually liberating once you accept it. You stop waiting to arrive at some future state of completion. You stop judging yourself for not being finished yet. You recognize that practice itself is the point, not some imaginary endpoint beyond it.

You're not broken and needing fixing. You're human and developing skills for navigating the inherent challenges of being human. Those challenges don't end, so the skill development doesn't end either.

The practice continues. And that's not a problem but it's just how living works.

You're Not Fucked

We started this book with you drowning in doom, convinced that everything was falling apart and you were powerless in the face of it. We walked through why your perception might be more distorted than reality itself, how your brain constructs narratives that become self-fulfilling, how attention and presence and connection and purpose all shape your experience more than you realized.

We looked at what's actually happening in the world including the real progress alongside the real problems, the genuine challenges that coexist with genuine possibilities. We explored how uncertainty is permanent but navigable, how action combats helplessness, how rest is resistance, how community is infrastructure.

You learned frameworks for rewriting narratives, building resilience, making decisions, finding meaning, and sustaining practice. You learned that you're not responsible for fixing everything, that your sphere of influence is real even if limited, that imperfect action beats perfect inaction.

And now you know: you're not fucked.

The world has genuine problems. You face real difficulties. Uncertainty persists. Suffering exists. None of that has changed.

What's changed is your relationship to those realities. You're not drowning in them anymore. You're swimming. Sometimes barely, sometimes gracefully, but swimming nonetheless. You have tools, perspectives, practices, and community to help you navigate what comes.

You're not fucked. You're here, you're trying, you're learning, you're adapting, you're growing. You're engaging with difficulty rather than being destroyed by it. You're finding meaning in struggle, connection in isolation, purpose in chaos, hope in uncertainty.

You're not fucked. You're alive in difficult times, doing your best with what you have, building capacity to handle what comes, contributing what you can from where you are.

You're not fucked. You're human. And that's enough.

Keep Going

The practice continues because life continues. The challenges will keep coming because that's what life does. And you'll keep navigating them because that's what you do.

Some days you'll do it well. Some days you'll barely survive it. Some days you'll forget everything and have to remember again. Some days you'll help someone else. Some days you'll need help yourself.

All of that is the practice. All of that is being human. All of that is enough.

You have what you need to keep going. Not everything you wish you had. Not perfect certainty or guaranteed outcomes. But enough tools, enough perspective, enough resilience, enough connection to navigate what comes.

So keep going. Keep practicing. Keep adapting. Keep starting again when you forget. Keep helping others when you can. Keep asking for help when you need it.

Keep engaging with your life instead of just consuming information about other people's lives. Keep showing up for what matters to you. Keep building the world you want to inhabit, one choice at a time, one practice at a time, one connection at a time.

The practice continues.

And so do you.

Not fucked. Not fixed. Not finished.

Just here. Still going. Still growing. Still human.

That's all you need to be.

Now close this book and go live.

About the Author

You know all you need to know about former journalist Zeke Maye after reading his book, in particular, the introduction. Zeke isn't on any social media platforms and never will be. He suggests you do the same.